PURPLE PARABLES

SNIPPETS FROM LIFE

SANDY GOFORTH

WESTBOW
PRESS*
A DIVISION OF THOMAS NELSON
& ZONDERVAN

WestBow Press books may be ordered through booksellers or by contacting:

WestBow Press
A Division of Thomas Nelson & Zondervan
1663 Liberty Drive
Bloomington, IN 47403
www.westbowpress.com
1 (866) 928-1240

ISBN: 978-1-9736-6921-0 (sc)
ISBN: 978-1-9736-6922-7 (hc)
ISBN: 978-1-9736-6920-3 (e)

Library of Congress Control Number: 2019909706

Print information available on the last page.

WestBow Press rev. date: 08/02/2019

To my husband, Dan, who has always prodded and guided me toward getting these stories published. And for his help with cooking, cleaning, and a lot of things he didn't need to do; his helpful and kind attitude allowed me writing time. Further, to my children, Rolland W. Lawrenz, Monika L. Snyder, Heidi L. McKeever, and Erika L. Hayes. They all have such creative skills and talents and have blessed and inspired my life immeasurably. Most importantly, to God be all glory and honor for providing His son as my Savior.

NOTE

The inspiration for *Purple Parables*: *Snippets from Life* is Jenny Joseph's poem, "When I Am Old." I so related to this poem and felt free to pursue my passion for writing. Thus, *Purple Parables: Snippets from Life* began to percolate throughout my journals. In these humble little tales, a bigger story came into focus—the wonderful story of how the Holy Trinity speaks to us through our experiences, provided we let them. These snippets are family stories, opinions, and thoughts of an aging woman. It is my desire that you will be inspired and find joy in what the Lord reveals through these stories.

NOTE

The inspiration for *Purple Parables: Snippets from Life* is Jenny Joseph's poem, "When I Am Old." I so related to this poem and felt free to pursue my passion for writing. Thus, *Purple Parables: Snippets from Life* began to percolate throughout my journals. In these humble little tales, a bigger story came into focus—the wonderful story of how the Holy Trinity speaks to us through our experiences, provided we let them. These snippets are family stories, opinions, and thoughts of an aging woman. It is my desire that you will be inspired and find joy in what the Lord reveals through these stories.

Contents

GOD'S PHONE CALL

We had two dogs: Twiggy and Bandit. They believed they absolutely had to go out between four thirty and five o'clock each morning. From their bedroom (the utility room), they started a soft, pathetic, annoying, relentless whining. When my babies grew up, I thought those top-of-the-morning wake-up calls would end. With these two, however, there was no such thing as sleeping in, and they never outgrew the habit.

For a long time, I found their early-morning antics aggravating. Then I discovered the thrill of watching spectacular sunrises. It is a time of peace, quiet, and solitude. The phones are silent, and no vehicles are flying down our dirt road while stirring up dust clouds. The stillness is broken only by the soft whinny of the horses, the crowing of the neighbor's rooster, the braying of wild burros, and the yip of a local coyote. As the sun breaks over the mountains, the bunnies and quail skitter across the yard. If I'm lucky, I'll see an owl or two returning to their roost. More importantly, it is a wonderful time to talk with God.

You will note I wrote "talk with God," because to talk *to* someone infers no response from the other party, but to talk *with* someone is a conversation. On one particular morning, I told God I felt overwhelmed, tired, and anxious. I told Him how I never had enough time to finish all the things I needed or wanted to finish. I sat there quietly waiting for Him to respond. I drank another cup of coffee, looked around at His beautiful creation, and still received no clear impressions. Finally, I gave up and went in the house, turned on the radio, and sat down at my computer. I found two emails from friends online. Each had separately sent me messages about modern-day lifestyles and how Satan works to defeat our walk with the Lord.

One message told of how Satan sets about to break our spirit by limiting our time with God. His plan is insidious. He employs many wily ways to distract us. First, he tempts us to *spend, spend, spend* and *borrow, borrow, borrow.* To fulfill our obligations, he persuades mothers and wives to work outside the home and forces husbands to work long hours to pay for debt-filled lifestyles. In so doing, there is less and less left for quality time as a family. As the family fragments, our homes are no longer sanctuaries; instead, they become pressure cookers. It used to be that riding in a car was a haven away from the distractions of life. Now Satan overstimulates by enticing us to play the radio, CDs, or DVDs (in some cars for the children's entertainment), play games on tablets, text friends, and of course check out the latest on Facebook. By doing so, he pounds our minds with twenty-four-hour blow-by-blow news coverage. He delights in filling our bookshelves, coffee tables, and side tables with magazines, catalogs, and other promotional materials offering false hope.

When we do try to find respite in some form of outdoor recreation, he'll be sure we do things in excess so that we return home exhausted. He would prefer that we go to concerts, sporting events, or amusement parks rather than take in a hike and reflect on God's glory as displayed in His marvelous creation. In the end, we are exhausted mentally, emotionally, physically, and spiritually. When we reach the lowest point of exhaustion, he opens his toolbox and pulls out the screwdrivers of pain: anxiety, frustration, discouragement, discontent, disappointment, and despair.

As I digested these messages, I realized that while I was not afflicted by all of Satan's tactics, some of his schemes did apply. I need to work on those that caused me to feel overwhelmed and discouraged. Isn't it amazing how God will answer your prayers, even by email? But the answer would not have been as clear had not Twiggy and Bandit forced me to spend some quiet time with the Lord. No longer will their whines be met with complaint. Instead, Twiggy and Bandit are the ringers of God's telephone each morning. That special time from five o'clock to six thirty is a peaceful bliss that sets the tone for the day. I am enjoying the beauty of silence, paying down old debt, and not creating new, and most of all, I take those early-morning hours to enjoy His handiwork, take a walk, water my trees, and talk with God.

Listen carefully. God's phone rings in mysterious ways.

As it is said, Today, if you hear his voice do
not harden your hearts as in rebellion.
—Hebrews 3:15 ESV

THE SMELL OF ROSES OR
THE STINK OF A STY

When we are living on a fast track, often we are admonished to take time to smell the roses. This sounded like good advice. My stress level was pretty high. I had a free day and thought it might be fun to spend it people watching and meditating. To start this utopian day, I stopped at Walmart to pick up some munchies (an absolute necessity for such an occasion).

I plopped down on a bench at the front of the store, figuring it would be a good place to people watch. Over the next hour, I watched as customers meandered in and rushed out. There was an abundance of women and grandmothers with children. Many offered bribes for good behavior. The next biggest group included retired couples. They were mostly two groups: the ones holding hands and those with one partner walking five paces ahead of the other. Because it was a school day, only a few hooky-playing teenagers ventured in. They kept their heads down with hoodies pulled forward in hopes of being inconspicuous as they looked furtively over their shoulders. Then there were the men who swaggered with a deliberate gait, obviously on a serious mission. And finally, there were the time killers who were easy to spot because they had no packages.

Some were clean; many were not. Some had smiles, but most went without. I overheard so much foul language. Has our language regressed to when you are in doubt of what to say or when you can't think of anything to say, use dirty words? My mother always said that profanity was the sign of a lazy mind. I agree.

With dismay, I watched rude people do rude things. I overheard couples fighting, watched as a child's arm was nearly pulled from its socket, and saw another child throw a tantrum over a quarter for a ride on a stationary motorcycle. It's definitely a shove-first, grab-first, me-first world. Is "Respect" now just the title of a song? When I left, I wondered if this was truly a cross section of our society. If so, there was more stink of a sty than the smell of roses in my day so far.

Maybe I expected too much and needed a time of meditation. I decided my front porch best fit the bill.

From there, an unobstructed view of blue and purple mountains frosted with white, frothy clouds filled me with wonder. I could enjoy the magnificent desert landscape, complete with a variety of critters. I poured an iced tea and went outside to meditate. Surely, the smell of roses would engulf me here.

After about thirty minutes of appreciating God's creation, I saw a dust cloud rising from the road and soon heard the rumble of an engine. Within a few seconds, a desert rapist (a.k.a. an oversized truck outfitted to carry off the mighty saguaros that have lived in this valley for centuries) rolled past. Once again, "mo' money" spoke louder than the desert's grandeur. After all, the rape of the desert is big business. We simply move the cactus around, because those who have previously raped property now want the cactus back and are willing to pay a lot for Arizona flora. Suddenly, there was an ear-shattering boom. I thought, *There they go again, dynamiting. I guess no roses are blooming here after all.*

Obviously, this "smelling the roses" thing was not what it was cracked up to be. Disappointed and discouraged, I sat in my living room. My eyes fell upon my Bible, my source of joy and encouragement. I really needed to read it because I felt so bummed. As I read, it became clear that the things I found so disturbing and tragic were not unfamiliar problems. The sty of sin, corruption, and pain are old problems that stink up our world.

When we do stop to smell the roses, we should first look to the Rose of Sharon, Jesus Christ. For when we meditate upon this Rose, our view is lifted from the sty of humankind's inhumanity, greed, and pride to the glorious spirituality of the soul.

Yes, it took some meandering, but I found the Rose. I took some time to meditate on His Word, filled my heart with the fragrance of His love, and the rest of my day was wonder filled.

I am the Rose of Sharon, The Lily of the Valley.
—Song of Solomon 2:1 NIV

PASSIONATE PROFESSIONS

By profession, my dad was an engineer. By passion, my dad was an artist. He worked hard, and his boss considered him "top drawer" at this job. He excelled and took immense pride in his work.

When my dad was in his early fifties, he had a series of serious heart attacks. In those days, there was a mandatory eight-week recuperation time before returning to work after a heart attack. During this downtime, Dad did little else but paint. He said he felt more alive painting than just lying around resting.

Eventually, he eagerly left on a Monday morning, anxious to get back to the normalcy and activity he had known for more than twenty-five years.

When he returned that evening, however, he seemed uncharacteristically quiet. Mom probed and prodded, wanting to know about his first day back at work. He responded, "It was okay."

Over the next few months, he continued going to work, but the spring in his step slipped away. Even though released by his doctor, his natural energy seemed sapped. In retrospect, he was probably suffering from depression, but to his family, we knew only that something was out of kilter. He spirit was restless and wandering, unfocused.

One day, he read in the paper that there was an open amateur art show at one of the malls, and the promoters were soliciting local talent to set up shop and offer their paintings for sale. Mom lacked her usual supportive spirit as she worried that this stress would only overwhelm him. He quickly took charge and convinced her this was what he wanted to do and admonished her not to worry so much.

In the weeks leading up to the show, Dad painted furiously. Often, he would come home from work and take his supper plate into his studio. He produced several small paintings and a couple of large ones. Then his engineering mind started to whirl as to how to best display his work. The next day, he began building an elaborate artist booth for the show.

On opening day, he got up at three o'clock in the morning to pack the car, loading everything into its specific place. (If you know an engineer, you can appreciate this.) Yes, Dad's color returned, his stride was that of a young man, and his shoulders no longer slumped.

For three days, he sat in that elaborate booth, talked with hundreds of people, and didn't sell one painting. For Dad, it became a challenge. He sought out the promoter and asked where the next show would be held and how he could get in. Thus, he started on a circuit of art shows and sales. He and Mom would go almost every weekend to some shopping mall, set up the booth, and hope to sell his paintings. One interesting sidebar, neither he nor Mom never missed a Sunday at church. They took turns staffing the booth. You see, Dad believed that God always came first.

Within a few months, he made a huge decision. He unequivocally chose to leave his job. No longer did he care about benefits, money, or prestige. He decided to follow his mending heart and finally do something he wanted to do.

From that time forward, he got up early, never seemed to tire, and painted all day. Days flew by, and Dad seemed to have found his own fountain of youth. Most of all, he loved the freedom of being able to do what he loved and being at home with Mom. As it turned out, his second career turned out to be quite profitable.

After several years, he had another heart attack. One day while he recuperated, we had one of the extra-special father-daughter talks. I asked him if he had any regrets. He thought for a moment and said, "No regrets, but I do wish I had followed my passion earlier in life."

How many of us feel the same way? God has so blessed each of us with enormous gifts, talents, and abilities. He inserts a passion in us to best use His gifts. For some, these gifts are thrown away, not nurtured, or even ignored. Fortunate is the person who recognizes His blessings, willingly follows His voice, and then cultivates His gifts. In so doing, they find a passionate profession. This must be one of life's most rewarding events because life becomes simpler, work is no longer work, and there is a sense of fulfillment not otherwise available. Most importantly, we glorify our heavenly Father by fulfilling His will for our lives.

Oh, to pursue that passionate profession. Now, there is something to contemplate. About twenty years ago, I, too, found my passionate profession, and three of my dad's grandchildren are currently following their passionate professions. The fourth one has always pursued his passion, even as it has changed from time to time.

Daddy … you left a tremendous legacy.

Keep your life free from the love of money, and
be content with what you have, for He has said, "I
will never leave you, nor will I ever forsake you."
—Hebrews 13:5 ESV

GRATITUDE ON STEROIDS

Often, wonderful stories begin in sadness or personal tragedy. This story begins with some truly wonderful friends, Ray and Lois. We, along with Ray and Lois, were part of a small group that met weekly to study God's Word. They were a unique couple. They were the "ready Freddys" of our group. First to volunteer for group work to help other people in need. They did everything from helping a lady who was living in squalid conditions to being a source of encouragement to others, ourselves included. We were going through a particularly difficult time financially and health wise, while also dealing with some family issues. Ray and Lois came alongside us.

A few years later, Ray started mentioning that he was having back pain. As the weeks progressed, his pain increased, and it was discovered he had a football-size malignant tumor on his kidney, and from there, the overall diagnosis was angiosarcoma. This was in September. Within just a couple of months, he was bedridden. As people gathered to visit Ray, a friend from work brought Ray and Lois a book, *1,000 Gifts: A Dare to Live Fully Right Where You Are* by Ann Voskamp. It is a writer's dream to write something that will encourage or touch a heart in some small way that will help the reader. And it did.

Ray's disease continued to take its toll, and it wasn't long before he needed to be in hospice and finally moved to an inpatient facility. The days grew longer for Lois as she spent ten to fourteen hours per day by his side. After reading Voskamp's book, she decided to try her hand at journaling. The idea of saying thank you to God was a positive way of turning her angst and fear into trust, obedience, and praise. Interestingly, the journal she started was entitled *Thank You*. And so she began. Each day, she looked for blessings. Likewise, Ray participated with his own journal, finding things for which he, too, could say thank you to God. Unfortunately, he couldn't keep up, as he soon grew too weak to write. Some days, she wrote nearly all day. And before she knew it, these thoughts were abundant, and she quickly reached one hundred entries. As the days passed in Ray's hospice room, she continued to faithfully write her thank yous to the Lord. She thanked Him for the sunrises, for the sunsets, for Ray sleeping peacefully, for her strength, and for her daughter's loving care. On March 14, she took a walk and returned to his room around noon. She sat down to write, and to her amazement, she wrote her thousandth entry. Ray passed peacefully around three thirty that afternoon into the arms of his Savior. He was jubilantly celebrating with the Lord.

That could have been the end of the story. But it isn't. Over the years since Ray's death, Lois continued with her journaling. These thank-you notes have become a way of life and have actually enabled Lois to come into a ministry at her church, with words of wisdom and encouragement to those who are lost, hurting, seeking, or desirous of making changes in their lives. Her life has a new meaning, joy, and happiness she never thought she would feel again after Ray died.

You might be interested to know she is now at eighteen thousand thank-you notes to the Lord. She has taken this very special venue born in a time of sorrow and let it explode in beautiful, sweet blooms of praise to the Lord. What a sweet aroma to the Lord. Lois, you are an inspiration to many. You truly do embrace a sense of gratitude on steroids.

They are to stand every morning to thank and
to praise the Lord, and likewise at evening.
—1 Chronicles 23:30 NASB

DIVIDED WE FALL

In the late 1950s, during dinner conversation, my father and our pastor were discussing the state of America and the upcoming election. Unbeknownst to anyone sitting around the table, this became a very prophetic conversation. Why was this conversation so memorable to me?

At the time, I was a senior at Central High School and determined that my dream job was to be a speech writer and (or) congressional liaison. So, any discussion about my favorite topic always got my attention. Many learned men and women prophesied about America's future, but none hit the bull's-eye quite like the predictions of these two men.

Pastor Bill prophesied that the greatest challenge to the American way of life was not communism but secularism and the blossoming of the Islamic religion.

The second point made by my dad dealt with segregation—not racial or ethnic but the various news organizations and their competition between one another.

Dad jokingly told our pastor that in the future, national elections would be decided by a handful of news organizations via their influence on the electorate. Both of these prophecies were made in 1959—sixty years ago.

If you look at the first prophecy, it is obvious that secularism has taken foothold in our nation. In the past sixty years, we no longer pray in school, the Ten Commandments have been removed from public buildings, nativity scenes are under attack, babies in utero are not babies but fetuses (except in the case of homicide), and this list is only touching the surface. Revisionist historians believe the United States was not founded upon Christian beliefs and principles, despite the clear references in our founding documents, such as the Declaration of Independence and Constitution.

Perhaps a quick look at just a couple statements by our founding fathers would give us pause before quickly falling prey to the new history.

"It is impossible to rightly govern the world without God and the Bible," said George Washington.

"Whatever makes men good Christians, makes them good citizens," said Daniel Webster.

One of our greatest presidents, Abraham Lincoln, said, "I believe the Bible is the best gift God has ever given man. All the good from the Savior of the world is communicated through this book ... all things desirable to men are contained in the Bible."

Islamic extremists and terrorists have certainly changed our sense of security as a nation. Many liberal politicians (those who believe in liberty) have moved decidedly to the Far Left (which espouses socialistic/communistic principles) and are enacting laws that certainly threaten our way of life. For many years, we have described the United States as a melting pot of nationalities. This is untrue. A melting pot produces an assimilated population with all the members contributing to the goodness of the country. Unfortunately, it appears now that each nationality seeks to keep its own identity rather than take on the mantle of being defined as an American. They do not want to be assimilated, and instead, they wish to be defined by their own culture, dress, language, and so on. I fear they do not fully comprehend the meaning of the United States of America. We are becoming the Divisive States of America.

Finally, Dad's prophecy that elections would be influenced and thereby controlled by the media is coming true. The battle for the heart of ordinary Americans is being waged by America's demigod: media—written, film, television, and digital.

For several years, I followed my theory for predicting the winner of national elections. Simply watch the nightly news and see what pictures of candidates they use in their news stories. The favored candidate will be smiling, kissing babies, looking very presidential, senatorial, or congressional. The unfavored candidate will look tired, haggard, and disheveled, caught tripping down the stairs or in any other unflattering pose. Watch for yourselves.

Are you already tired of the viciousness of the political rhetoric that bombards us daily? In recent elections, the elements of the vulgarity, vitriol, and decline of truth rose to a level never before approached. Gentlemanly or ladylike behavior has been replaced by crudeness, splitting the hair of truth, and vicious verbal one-liners. Inflamed party passions have reached the point of pure hatred. The result is the radicalization of our society. In these difficult days, we should remember that united we stand, divided we fall.

Every person is to be in subjection to the governing authorities. For there is no authority except from God, and those which exist are established by God.
—Romans 13:1 NASB

HARD OF HEARING

Over the past few years, hearing has become an issue for both my husband and myself. Being in our truly senior years, I consider it fortunate that, until recently, we have escaped the seriousness of this issue.

Apparently, the politically correct way to say it is one has "diminished" hearing. It is a progressive problem that does not get better with age. It has an unobtrusive start—just an occasional repeating of a word or phrase to someone.

Depending on one's sense of humor, the next step is making corny jokes about "clean the wax out of your ears," "your ears ain't a potato patch ... quit digging," and "always knew there wasn't anything in there." You get the picture. From there, things start to go rapidly downhill. Before you know it, you start to watch captioned television or, in my husband's case, no sound, just the captioned words. He always muted the television whenever I spoke to him. Then came the troubling time. I noticed that he watched people more intently. He was unintentionally learning to lip-read. I watched as he grew more silent and started to withdraw at family gatherings and in conversations with friends. It was time to stop playing the game of "Oh, quit it. I can hear you." I responded, "Yeah, right," to which he made no reply.

Finally, after more than one heart-to-heart conversation, he admitted that he "guessed" his hearing wasn't as good as it had been. We started looking for the perfect *hearing-assistance device*—note, not *hearing aids.*

He was very fortunate to have a good audiologist. The doctor made him feel comfortable and assured him he was not alone with this issue. He carefully guided him through the various steps in selecting an audio-assistance device that would best serve his needs. What a transformation! My husband was once again engaged, his sense of humor returned, and the television volume did not need to be at thirty-five. Life was good until I developed tinnitus. You know, that incessant noise in one's ears. A low, persistent ringing or buzzing. I didn't realize it at the time that this too is diminished hearing. I kept it to myself and, for sure, did not mention it to my husband. I have yet to make an appointment with the audiologist because I don't think of it as a big deal. Sound familiar?

Keeping all of this in mind, the other morning while I did my devotions, prayer, and Bible study, I asked, quite simply, "What can I do to be of service for you, Lord? I am listening." As I continued my study, a thought whizzed through my head, *Maybe you are hard of hearing.* That set me off in a flurry of thought processes.

Over many years, I have dabbled with writing. I was fortunate to have a couple of children's books, a few magazine articles, a newspaper column, and a contribution to a nonfiction book published. I cannot say it was a full-blown passion, but I definitely had a desire to be a writer. I always wanted to share my faith in such a way that would give pause and encouragement to the reader and lead them to recognize God's presence in their life through everyday happenings.

When I retired from leading a quilt ministry at church and quit teaching quilting, I was floundering about like a cat looking for an elusive mouse, dashing here and there and never quite snagging the prize. Community Bible Study has been my lifeline. It has and continues to be a daily process wherein I am blessed. Yet I still have tinnitus, and there really was another voice to hear.

As I explored that random thought throughout the day and evening and over the next several days, I began to see just how my hearing was affected by this incessant buzzing. Gone was quietness! While I could lose track of it when I was concentrating or focused, it was always there. As the days rolled by, I was convinced the Lord was telling me to quit avoiding my desire and go for it. There were many signs over the previous five years, wherein He showed me that He wanted me to be a storyteller for Him. I was just too hard of hearing and preoccupied with trying to drown out the buzz.

Maybe I wasn't listening; maybe I was afraid of what He had to say; maybe I didn't use a top-of-the-line assisted-listening device (a.k.a. prayer). Perhaps I thought I was too old to contribute anything of real value. You might have heard it said, "Well, I guess He's not done with me yet." There is immense truth in that statement, my friends. As long as we walk this earth and draw breaths, He has a mission for us. What's yours? How's your hearing? Do you need an assisted-listening device? You know where to find one. Go for it!

Whatever you do, do all to the glory of God.
—1 Corinthians 10:31 NASB

Job Satisfaction

Have you noticed there appears to be an increasing dissatisfaction in the workplace? There is more rudeness than kindness and helpfulness. Last week at the market, an older woman using a walker stopped a clerk and inquired about where an item was located. The clerk literally scowled at her and said, "Don't ask me. I work in produce." There was no offer to find someone else to assist her. Later that day, a call to a plumbing company inquiring when the plumber might arrive led to the customer-service representative's response, "Your guess is as good as mine. You're on the list, and he'll get there when he can."

On the flip side, however, at the JoAnns, Etc. store in Ahwatukee, Arizona, there is a clerk who truly appears to enjoy her job. She is helpful and willing to go the extra mile to make sure your questions are answered. Regardless of how long the line, she is calm and relaxed. She makes each customer feel welcome and special.

Katherine Graham once asked, "To love what you do and feel that it matters—how could anything be more fun?" Given that no job is perfect or enjoyable all the time, it is possible for us to derive satisfaction from what we do. We spend eight or more hours of the day working. It is really important to enjoy what we are doing. Otherwise, life will be miserable for half of our waking time and rife with frustration and unhappiness.

There are three key elements that can bring satisfaction to our work. It is about changing your attitude about the foibles of coworkers, thinking about why you are working, and finally, recognizing that what you are doing reflects on or helps others.

First, we should look around our workplaces and recognize that each person there is a child of God. Try to look at them through God's eyes. He looks for the good in His children. Can we write down one good trait about every one of our coworkers? Can we pay each person with whom we work a genuine compliment? When our focus changes, we might be surprised at what we learn about someone else and what impact we might have on their lives.

Second, recognize that even though we work for our employers, we are, in fact, working for ourselves. We are working to maintain our family and our possessions, and more importantly, we are preserving and building our self-esteem. It is essential that we feel good about what we do. We need to take pride in each and every task. If we set daily goals regarding our productivity for the day, we will enhance our sense of accomplishment, which naturally leads to feeling that we made a contribution to our company. Identify how what we do is a value to *our* company.

Third, know that what we do benefits others. For some people, this is the intangible element. Every job, no matter how menial, has potential to help someone else. Maybe we will find a way, either through our church or other charity, to reach and be of service to someone. It helps when we realize that everything we have, earn, or are given belongs to God. It is our responsibility to be a good steward of our resources. Reflect on what we do and seek to find out how it will benefit someone else. For example, if you are a childcare worker, recognize that you have been entrusted to care for another parent's most treasured blessings. If you are an assembly-line worker, think about the finished product and how it will impact people's lives.

Understanding these three elements about who we work with, why we work, and who will benefit from our work gives more meaning to our jobs. When we have meaning and purpose, we will have enjoyment. As our attitudes change, so will those of our coworkers and the public with whom we come in contact. What a difference we can make if we exchange rudeness for kindness.

But as for you brothers, do not
grow weary of doing good.
—2 Thessalonians 3:13 NASB

DOING NOTHING
AVAILS NOTHING

Random thoughts pass through my head. In July, I wanted to buy a turkey breast for dinner. There were none. Why is it most of us only have turkey twice a year? Are turkeys harder to grow than chickens, beef, or pigs?

This rabbit trail led me to thinking about Thanksgiving preparations. It starts with scurrying to the garage and attic to pull out those holiday totes and boxes. Inside were treasures of good china, silver, crystal, and beautifully crocheted lace tablecloths. Most of these beautiful things belonged to my mother. Every year, I go through the hallways of memories when I pull these items from hibernation. Not to be cliché, but a funny thing happened on my way to Memoryville. Rather than remembering the many gorgeous dinners, my thoughts turned to the year we had the most unusual, nontraditional Thanksgiving.

My father was a conservative aeronautical engineer, and his reputation for accuracy, preciseness, and attention to detail was legendary at work and at home. He believed in keeping family traditions, and he relished the holidays and always made sure all the details were covered. For example, we erected the Christmas tree on December 10 each year. Without fail, we mailed all Christmas cards on December 12. He was just as precise about the menu for Thanksgiving. Dinner included turkey, ham, dressing, mashed potatoes, gravy, cranberry salad, green beans, corn, sweet potatoes, and, of course, Mother's lime and ginger Jell-O, homemade rolls, and pumpkin and pecan pies.

His Thanksgiving task was to set the table (there were only three of us, as all family lived out of state). He did so with almost religious fanaticism. It was beautiful with fresh spider mums, baby pumpkins, and fruit for the centerpiece. It looked like something out of *Better Homes and Gardens* magazine. Mother was an excellent cook; her turkey perfectly browned, fluffy light rolls, moist ham, mashed potatoes without lumps, smooth gravy, and pies from heaven. Yes, we always had that Norman Rockwell Thanksgiving dinner.

You can imagine our shock when about two weeks before Thanksgiving, Dad announced that we were changing the Thanksgiving menu. That year, we feasted on barbequed hot dogs, potato chips, pickles, potato salad, baked beans, and pecan pie. (Pecan was his favorite pie, and nothing and no one would cause him to give it up.) He said we would use paper products. For days, Mother stewed, fretted, and worried. As far as she was concerned, this was pure craziness. Dad insisted, and Dad prevailed.

On that Thanksgiving, Dad set the table with a paper tablecloth. For a centerpiece, he used one of those fan-out paper turkeys, and he set the table with paper plates and plastic table service. Mother was convinced his cheese had slipped off his cracker.

The day progressed, and we sat down to this meager and simple meal. Mother barely contained her frustration, and Dad appeared to be having a simply wonderful time, oblivious of her distress. I didn't know what to think. At last, this strained day ended with no explanation forthcoming from Dad.

Years went by, and no one ever mentioned Dad's one day of lunacy. Each year thereafter, as the holidays approached, Mother and I talked about it, yet we never asked him directly about our nontraditional feast. I guess we were afraid that he might once again lose his bearings and we'd have another odd Thanksgiving.

Later, as an adult, I finally asked him about that strange day. He started to laugh.

He said, "You remember that? I'd completely forgotten." I promptly told him that neither Mother nor I had forgotten, and, in fact, we thought about it every Thanksgiving. He apologized that his action had caused such "anguish." He told me that it started out as a charity thing and grew into this strange ministry. He and several of his friends used to gather for a breakfast Bible study. At one such meeting, they calculated the cost of the feast with all the trimmings and decided that instead of paying for such an elaborate feast for themselves, they would do the bare minimum and contribute the rest to the Salvation Army. They all agreed to keep this charity act anonymous and not share their good deed with anyone unless directly asked.

Yes, it was a bit strange and even odd, but the lesson was clear. Mom and I didn't face the issue when it first arose and avoided asking the simple question, "Why?" We let it happen, we stewed about it, we worried about it, but we *did nothing* about it. Yes, unintentionally, Dad taught me an important lesson. Doing nothing avails nothing.

While this was a very simplistic lesson, it is surprising how many times in life we do nothing because we are either fearful or lack understanding. The danger of doing nothing can deeply affect us in other areas of life.

For some, marriages disintegrate because people do nothing. They either stop or don't ask questions because they are afraid of or don't want to know the answers. Couples go their separate ways after doing nothing together.

When it comes to our eternal life, many people do nothing. Instead they stew, fret, and worry for years because they do not understand the Bible or are afraid to ask questions. Unfortunately, they will never experience the joy and peace of mind that come from knowing Jesus gave His life for our sins. They live in a guilt-ridden world.

Now is the time to resolve those questions and to *do something*! And for believers, it is time to unveil the mystery of the Gospel with those who are lost in the fog of misunderstanding.

The righteous is a guide to his neighbor, but
the way of the wicked leads them astray.
—Proverbs 12:26 NASB

ALOHA AND SWEET MANA

Traditionally, Valentine's Day is dedicated to lovers, but truly it is the day to honor *love* and all those people who have loved and nurtured us. Many loving people have richly blessed my life. So many, in fact, that I have not enough years left to write a valentine tribute for each one.

While living in Hawaii, I became enamored with Hawaiian culture and crafts, especially Hawaiian quilts. These quilts are unique and treasured works of art. Like the islands, they are spectacular, bold, vivid, yet graceful. Before long, I knew that I had to learn how to make these exquisite kapas (bed coverings). Little did I realize that learning to quilt would change my viewpoint of life.

I was lucky to take lessons from a master quilter, Mealii Kalama, a lay pastor at the famed Kawaiaha'o Church in Honolulu. Aunty Mealii, as she preferred to be called, was a humble, loving, and generous woman. Named as one of America's National Treasures of Folk Artists, she was a goodwill ambassador for Hawaii and Hawaiian quilts.

Each Thursday morning, fifty to seventy people gathered at the church to study Hawaiian crafts, one of which was Hawaiian quilting, under her tutelage. Filled with aloha (love) and a sweet mana (spirit), she moved through the large meeting hall, encouraging each person with a kind word or pat on the shoulder. Her hands, though gnarled by the ravages of arthritis, could still master a needle to show a beginner how to applique or make a tiny quilt stitch.

For Aunty, the entire quilt-making process was a spiritual journey. She taught that designing and making a quilt was an expression of God's creativity. Immensely talented and artistic, Aunty's designs reflected her love and service to God. Somewhere in each quilt, she inserted what she called her logo. All of her quilts contain an interwoven design of a young seedling, uncurling and rising to face the sun. She said that these seedlings represented our lives as we grow and mature to eventually rise to face God.

Often she spoke of the importance of showing aloha and using our sweet mana (spirit). She said we should work on our quilts only when we were happy. The recipient should feel the protection and warmth of our love. I might add these quilts can often take years to complete. Aunty reminded us that we can give no greater gift than a gift of ourselves. To give such a quilt to someone expresses our deep love for them. The journey is complete when it is given away. The quilt serves as an outward reminder of the warmth, comfort, and protection we receive from our Father and of His wonderful gift to us.

Yes, Aunty Mealii taught me how to quilt and so much more. Under her guidance, my faith was refreshed. I learned how to celebrate life and recognize the power of the Holy Spirit. Her words of encouragement helped me to accept new challenges. Most importantly, she taught me how to turn my face to the Father.

God's spirit flowed through Aunty to everyone with whom she had contact. She touched people's souls and helped them to see God's providence. She taught that our creativity mirrors God's presence in our lives. In tribute, when she passed away, the church overflowed with family, friends, students, and a spectacular array of priceless Hawaiian quilts. Her legacy lives on the hearts of those she touched and through beautiful masterpieces.

I miss Aunty, but in my mind, I can see her smile as she quilts with a golden needle. There are times when I think I feel her hand on my shoulder and hear her humming the old hymn, "There's a Sweet, Sweet Spirit in this Place."

Gracious words are a honeycomb, sweet
to the soul and healing to the bones.
—Prov. 16:24 NIV

OVER THE TOP OR BELOW THE BOTTOM

Recently I was invited to lunch and a live theatre performance of a new musical comedy. My husband and I have been longtime ticket holders at a local dinner theatre and love the arts, especially the live theatre and musicals. The beauty of the musicals lies in the fact that they have generally clean humor, great music, and dancing, and they tell a cute story. As a whole, they are uplifting, and rarely do you leave the theatre without a smile on your face. This group of creative people who are blessed with the trifecta of singing, dancing, and acting have my admiration.

This particular new musical opened with two men dressed as women. The outlandish style made the first appearance on stage quite funny. They performed their first song well, but after that, the show reached new lows in raunchiness. While the language was not vulgar (thank goodness), the balance of the performance was a tainted exposé of vulgarity in action. The humor was tasteless and filled with sexual overtones, innuendos, and graphic gyrations.

No doubt, the playwright thought the script was clever; it was not. I don't consider myself a prude, but making fun of an audience participant's religion coupled with off-color remarks was disconcerting. To watch as people were randomly picked from the audience, then squirmed and attempted to hide their embarrassment while being humiliated by these actors made me angry. Leaving the show was not really an option since I had come with several other ladies. I looked down the row of friends and saw raised eyebrows; it was obvious an air of distaste was blowing around us all.

So, why was the audience apparently so enthralled and having a grand time? I wondered, Have we really become such a crass society? When did it happen? Am I really blind to a mighty culture shift? Or were they laughing to cover their embarrassment? Did they know what was coming?

When I got home, I did some investigation. I watched some videos and found them funny, clever, and very benign.

Our culture is like a messy house. It takes a while to get in a mess, but after a while, we are unable to see the mess any longer, nor do we care. Or, in the best scenario, we are overwhelmed. Our culture is so anesthetized to the slippage of virtues of honesty, character, and integrity we no longer are aware they have been replaced with lies, ill repute, and unrighteousness. Probably most who attended the show had no idea of the depravity and amoral nature of the material. As for the rest, hopefully this show was below the bottom; they will reflect on what kind of humor is truly funny and what kind is tasteless and raunchy.

I am thankful, however, that I went to this disgusting show because it shined a light to look at the slippages and messes within my own sphere. Yes, it brought me to repentance, which is the place we all need to be—on our knees before the Lord.

For godly grief produces a repentance
that leads to salvation without regret,
whereas worldly grief produces death.
—2 Corinthians 7:10 ESV

It's the Little Things That Count

A few years ago, a group of friends surprised me with a birthday party. (Actually, the surprise was my age.) It wasn't a fancy affair but rather just good fellowship, some cake, and cards. Their thoughtfulness was overwhelming and was summed up in one of those "little" things that make a lasting difference in life. I doubt they even knew what a lifeline they threw to me that night.

Knowing that I love giraffes, a dear friend covered a tall tin box and lid with giraffe fabric. Tucked away inside were little notes written by my friends. Some wrote scripture verses, and others wrote funny or clever sayings or poems. They told me to randomly pull one of these pearls from the tin whenever I needed a lift.

Now, years later, I still have the magic tin with its messages of hope and encouragement. My tin sits on my desk, and every time I look at it, I smile. It is my personal genie in a bottle. I know all of the messages by heart, and the slips of paper are well worn, but I never tire of reading them.

We all have days when we feel lonely, dejected, disappointed, and frightened—sometimes with good reason, and other times for no reason. In recent years, there has been a meteoric rise in the number of people suffering from depression and anxiety. Many rely on mood-altering drugs as a quick fix for dealing with daily dilemmas.

When blue days assail me, there are times I don't want to share my problem or mood with anyone. Instead, I reach for my quick fix from my giraffe tin and know someone's loving thoughts await me.

It is amazing that with the variety of messages, the one I pull out is always perfect for the situation I face. Is there magic in these little notes? No, but it is uncanny that even after years, these notes still provide that extra-special lift needed.

The older one gets, the less important material gifts become. When I look back at the gifts I have received, the ones that left a lasting impression are those little things that showed someone really knew and cared for me. Most store-bought gifts either wear out or become dust catchers (and I certainly have enough of those), but that giraffe tin filled with encouragement holds a place of high esteem in my house.

The blessings in little gifts are not just for the recipient. The giver is also blessed in knowing that they have helped someone have a better day. There are a variety of ways to make these little gifts. Of course, you too could make a genie-in-a-bottle tin for a dear friend by passing around index cards and having others put their favorite scripture references on them. Often these references are a perfect launching point for much-needed meditation.

Other similar ideas would be as follows:

(1) Purchase an inexpensive diary or calendar and pass it amongst a birthday person's friends so they can jot down a thought for the day at the top of each page.

(2) If your friend has an email, take turns sending them daily or weekly notes with a joke or a famous quote. It doesn't have to be long, and it only takes a minute to send something as simple as "May God go with you today" or maybe a silly knock-knock joke.

(3) This idea requires a yearlong commitment, but the gift will be deeply treasured. Starting on your friend's birthday, keep

a diary yourself. Each day, enter your thoughts or a prayer for your friend. Then give it to them on their next birthday.

In this complex world, the goal should be to simplify life, return to our core values, and truly care for one another. Then, maybe the little genie in the bottle will not be labeled Prozac or Xanax but rather *love*. This quick fix will allow you to be a servant of Jesus and show the same care, compassion, empathy, and love He shows us daily.

Every good gift and every perfect gift is from above,
coming down from the Father of lights with whom
there is no variation or shadow due to change.
—James 1:17 ESV

A FRIEND

For a number of years, we lived in Seattle and were fortunate to live near Woodland Park Zoo. Twice weekly, the children and I went to the zoo. It was always a great outing ... until one day.

As we strolled along the paths between the animal enclosures, my two-year-old daughter, without any apparent provocation, started to scream hysterically. She pulled away and started to run in circles. She grabbed my legs and buried her head and sobbed uncontrollably. Whenever she peeked out, she started to scream again. I checked to see if she had been stung or bitten or if her clothing was pinching her. She appeared to be fine physically, but emotionally she was a wreck. Finally, she quieted and whimpered softly, until we started to move out onto another path. She screamed in terror. It was so frightening. Never before had she ever screamed and cried like this. It was obvious that something was terribly wrong and it was not a temper tantrum. Her screaming continued unbated for several minutes. Whatever was upsetting her struck a chord of pure panic in her mind and in mine.

Several people stopped and stared. I looked about frantically for a first aid station or for anyone who could help. A soft-spoken elderly gentleman left the crowd of onlookers, approached us, and asked if he could help. I explained I didn't know what was wrong. He slowly walked toward her, patted her head, and said, "I think she is afraid of her shadow. Let's take her inside out of the sun and see if she stops." We hurried to the nearby monkey house. Once inside, she immediately stopped crying and was all smiles again within just a couple of minutes. To test the theory, we went back outside in the sun, and within just a few seconds, she was screaming and crying.

So began a long journey of getting her to feel safe and accept the shadows she might see. For weeks, we pointed to shadows and said, "Friend." At last, she tentatively pointed to her shadow and said, "Friend." Shadows were now her friends.

It doesn't take much to see the analogy between a small child's fears and our grown-up fears producing problems that cast long shadows on our days. How we react to them is a key indicator of our ability to cope and our potential for success.

We've all known people who react to life's shadows much the same way my daughter did. They panic and lose all sense of direction and cognitive reasoning. Others choose to hide from their shadows. They live a life of avoidance and prefer to live very controlled and structured lives, choosing instead to perfect everything around them and thereby drive the shadows away. They rarely take any risks and wrap themselves in the cloak of insecurity. When a shadow falls across their path, they are ill-equipped to handle or cope with such a situation. They fall apart, unable to keep their equilibrium, and often recede from the experiences that normally produce a sense of well-being. They react to life rather than live life.

Another group ignores their shadows. While they are constantly aware of them, they mistakenly believe that if they ignore them long enough, they will go way. Like the afternoon shadows, their problems only look larger and longer. Their ostrich style of procrastination eventually leads to a near paralysis on inaction.

Successful people learn early on that they need not be afraid. They understand there always will be shadows and that they can be neither avoided nor hidden. They choose not to be governed by them but rather to deal with them.

It might seem foolish to say that life shadows can be called "friend," but we do have a friend, much like that elderly gentleman that helped my daughter that day so long ago. He knows our problems; He stands ready to help us, and He is always available. We need only ask for His help, be willing to listen to His counsel, and follow His guidance. In Him, we find refuge and knowledge to handle our obstacles. So, the next time a shadow looms on your horizon, just call out, "Friend."

The friendship of the Lord is for those who fear
him, and he makes known to them his covenant.
—Psalm 25:14 ESV

TECHNOLOGY AND HISTORY

Recently, while sorting through a closet, I found a box filled with old pictures, scraps of paper, postcards, and letters. Among these treasures, I found one of the hundreds of letters and postcards my mother mailed to me more than forty years ago. Her letters were both newsworthy and meandering. They recorded everyday occurrences, offered encouraging comments, and on occasion issued an admonition. My mother died forty years ago. As I reread her letter, it evoked powerful memories. I felt transported back in time as she wrote about her grandchildren who were still little tykes and how she framed a childish drawing from my son. She told of people and family who have since passed away. She wrote of church activities and everyday events, such as a good sale at Goldwater's Department Store. She penned her hopes and disappointments. Needless to say, Mother could get more on a postcard than most people can write in a letter. And I could still read her beautiful, extremely small script.

What a nugget of joy it is to receive a letter from a friend or a relative among the barrage of bills and junk mail. We feel special because we know the sender actually took time from their busy schedules to sit down, compose their thoughts, and write them down. The value of these letters is measured by how long we hold on to them. Rare is the person who reads a personal letter and immediately throws it in the trash. We usually read and reread these treasures. Sometimes, we tuck them away for another day.

Have you ever wondered what a historian would find if they were to attempt to reconstruct your life by letters, notes, or journals you have written, or from letters written to you? Would there be anything from which they could glean an insight as to who you were or what kind of a world you lived in?

At the heart of historical research is the use of primary sources. One such source is the letters or diaries written during the era being studied. Eloquent writing is not a criterion for a historical record. Most diaries and letters are filled with personal thoughts that flow without consideration for continuity. Rarely does the mind think of events in perfect chronological order or in flawless grammar. There are no rewrites of journals or diaries. They are merely observations and expressions of a journalist.

Consider the historic significance of *The Diary of Anne Frank* or the journals from the Lewis and Clark expedition. Or, where would we be without the great writings of the Bible? The writers provided us with such history and hope for the future. Think of the encouragement you receive from the Psalms of David, the wisdom gained from Proverbs, the rich history found in Exodus, the message of salvation given in John, and the hope delivered in the letters of Paul. The endurance of these writings point to their relevance for our lives.

Due to technology, we are no longer teaching cursive writing in school. This particular loss is significant inasmuch as handwriting tells a great deal about the writer, including their mood when they wrote their note. It will be so much easier for you to stop forgery of documents because cursive writing makes your signature valuable. When we dash off those emails, they are much less personal and probably less attentive to detail. Yet we need to keep current with technology, or we will soon be left out of communication with the world, but we can and should continue with personal, handwritten accounts. In the future, a historian might sift through our writing, searching for clues of what life was like, what was important to us. We cannot trust that digital communication or videos will fill that void. Anything digital can be lost.

Keeping an email record is highly unlikely. Unless you are immensely well organized and take appropriate safeguards, messages of love, blessings shared, and encouragement given can be lost in the vastness of the internet. Why not write a letter or thank-you note, or keep a journal. It is important, and who knows—you might get a letter to put in your treasure chest. There is something special about looking at a loved one's handwriting years after they have passed. Technology can't replace this timeless connection.

Let such a person consider this, that what
we are in word by letters when absent, such
persons we are also in deed when present.
—2 Corinthians 10:11 NASB

How Does Your
Garden Grow?

Oh, how I love gardens, all kinds—vegetable, floral, or herbal. Unfortunately, the feeling is not mutual. My family learned long ago to take pity on houseplants and never get me one as a gift. It is a known fact that with little or no effort, I can kill a cactus.

My gardening ability is seriously lacking. I am totally inept and without much hope of ever having a fruitful and productive garden. I give the plants either too much water or not enough. I overfeed or starve them. I expose them to too much or too little sunlight. I either prune them too severely or let the suckers grow. I bomb the bugs with too much pesticide or choose a fertilizer with the wrong pH (whatever that is). Finally, I get frustrated, throw my hands up, walk away, and let the weeds take over. After all, some weeds are quite pretty. I can't kill them.

Regardless of my many failures, I still get this gardening urge. So, with encouragement from friends and family, I vowed, once more, to bed and care for yet another garden. This time it would be successful. I read gardening books and magazine articles, studied package labels, and drove nursery workers crazy with dozens of questions. Then a dear friend said, "You don't learn to garden by reading books. The secret to a successful garden is simply daily care."

What a revelation! There wouldn't be many weeds to pull if I pulled them each day. If it started to wilt, give it water. If a few leaves began to look like Swiss cheese, look out for a pest. Then take proactive steps to eliminate it.

As I planted my seeds, I contemplated her words and thought of how often such a simple statement can be applied to our spiritual lives. What about our minds? Isn't the mind merely a living garden of thoughts, fruited with wisdom, love, and a caring nature? It is kind of scary when I considered the garden of my mind. When was the last time it was weeded? Had it been watered or nurtured recently? Is it bearing fruit? Or, are the plants of thoughts being choked out by weeds, dying for a lack of water, or chewed up by pests—pests of anger, depression, frustration, or impatience?

As surely as I must daily attend to my vegetable garden, I must cultivate the garden of my mind. Maybe today, the weeds of hatred, anger, selfishness, and greed need to be pulled. My garden needs to be watered with the wisdom and hope from God's Word and nurtured with His love. I need His protection to shade me from scorching and deadly rays of evil and bad influences. When necessary, I should diligently prune away the dead wood of old habits and look for those pests that insidiously destroy the plants. I need to stimulate new growth by cultivating the soil with knowledge and rotate my crops to avoid being stuck in old ruts. I must allow the soil to rest and regenerate. And, finally, as my seedlings mature, I must be willing to allow them to be transplanted.

By applying the gardening principle of daily care to both our physical and mental gardens, we are assured of being fruitful rather than barren. It is known that we will reap what we sow, but along with this fact lies another trust: if we are careful tenders of our gardens, we can also increase our yield. Who knows? Maybe this time I will get a good crop of red, juicy tomatoes and new souls for the Lord.

For as the earth brings forth its sprouts,
And as a garden causes the things
sown in it to spring up,
So the Lord God will cause righteousness and praise
To spring up before all the nations.
—Isaiah 61:11 NASB

THE GOLDEN
THREADS OF LIFE

Every time I smell strawberries, I'm reminded of how Grandpa filled my insatiable appetite for this fruit.

Every time I taste homemade noodles, I am reminded of Grandma's flour-smudged face.

Every time I read a story to a child, I recall my grandpa's wonderful stories and tall tales.

Every time I set patches together for a quilt, I recall my grandma's gnarled hands showing me how to sew scraps together.

Every time I hear "Onward Christian Soldiers," I hear my grandpa singing in his garden.

Every time I read Psalm 121, I hear my grandma reciting her breakfast prayer.

In the tapestry of my life, the golden threads were woven by my grandparents.

Hillary Clinton said it takes a village to raise a child, but in truth, it takes a family to raise a child. It takes the full family of father, mother, grandparents, aunts, and uncles. While the village may have an effect, God ordained the family for the purpose of instilling values and morals. Relinquishing familial responsibilities and expecting unrelated individuals (with the exception of adoptive family units) to fill the gap is at the core of why we are witnessing the breakdown of society. No one can love your children more than you and your family.

Like never before, today's society beckons extended family involvement. In a world where spiritual and moral values are challenged, manipulated, and blatantly overthrown, raising and protecting children should be our first concern.

Unfortunately, children are bombarded with issues of adult problems. They are exposed to a host of these issues—violence, death, gangs, drugs, drive-by shootings, sexual predators, separation, divorce, and now the uncertainty of living through the school day. They are growing up in a climate of fear. Grandparents can offer refuge where children can be insulated from the outside world.

Grandparents have the time to listen, to share life's experiences and pass on tidbits of wisdom. Grandchildren love nothing more than to hear stories of things that happened before they were born. My grandchildren begged for stories about their parents. Much to their surprise, they learned that their parents faced many of the same challenges they do. Unbeknownst to the child, these stories are carefully chosen because they contain lessons of meeting challenges, having respect, and understanding unconditional love.

In God's infinite wisdom, He provided that there be six significant adults in the child's life—their parents and two sets of grandparents. Whether a child is being raised in a traditional or nontraditional setting, the one constant factor is the grandparents' stability. As our moral and spiritual fabric is stretched and sometimes torn, grandparents offer a spiritual haven. Grandparents stand as a testament of a tried and tested faith. They know the power of prayer and have witnessed God's handiwork in their lives. For some families, going to church is no longer a priority. Here is a wonderful opportunity for grandparents to fill that spiritual gap. By reading Bible stories and taking children to Sunday school, they help plant the seeds for salvation.

Far too many children and adolescents are frightened, discouraged, and depressed. When things go awry, the children are first to shoulder the blame. Many hold their feeling at bay because they fear upsetting or disappointing their parents. It is at times like these when grandparents can make a significant contribution, reinforcing the crucial messages of hope and faith.

Our job is to be *grand*parents. With that title comes an enormous responsibility. Being a grandparent is life's last work. Just as a flower buds, then blooms, it also fades and drops its petals. This last stage of flowering is the most important, because it is then that the seed drops—to raise up the next generation.

But as for you, continue in what you have
learned and have become convinced of, because
you know from whom you learned it.
—2 Timothy 3:14 NIV

CRAM FEST

Weekends—forty-eight hours of bliss, two glorious days to slow down, relax, and be refreshed. Not! All week, we look forward to the weekend. We have high expectations of having some time to ourselves. Unfortunately, more and more weekends are simply extensions of the work week.

With the advent of the home office, precious personal time is used to catch up on unfinished work tasks. We live each day by our organizers or planners. Everything we do is scheduled and time slotted, seven days a week. Isn't it amazing with all of the modern conveniences and timesaving devices, it seems we have less time than our parents and grandparents? Gone are those lazy days of napping, reading, playing games, or just plain resting. Instead, our weekends are filled with errands, shopping, yard work, chauffeuring children to and from sporting events, piano or dance lessons, laundry, and housework. For most of us, weekends should be called a cram fest.

We pay a high price for our fast-paced lifestyle. The lack of rest exacts its toll as more people than ever before suffer from depression, job dissatisfaction, chronic irritability, and frustration. Topping the list of maladies associated with such an overload is an out-of-control life filled with guilt. When we do stop and take a few minutes for ourselves, we invariably cancel out any pleasure, joy, or benefit by thinking of things that need to be done. Have you ever sat down to read a book, and within a few minutes, you find your mind wandering to some unfished task? As the guilt moves in, the pleasure is obscured.

Have you ever wondered why we love rainy days (which are far and few between in the desert)? Inclement weather allows us, without guilt, to curl up with a good book, take a nap, watch a movie, or play a game. Rainy days bring out our nesting and resting instincts. We seek shelter and a place to escape from worldly concerns, a place to rest. These things can't be found in the mall, the grocery store, the car, or someone else's house. They are found at home. Unfortunately (or fortunately), it doesn't rain every Sunday.

Past generations understood the value of rest. They acknowledged God's grand design and respected the value of a day of rest. My parents made sure that Sundays were restful family days. There were no shopping excursions to the mall or other task-related errands. Mother prepared Sunday dinners on Saturday to avoid cooking on Sunday. She placed her prepared meal in the oven or in the crockpot before we left for church, and when we returned, dinner was ready. Sunday afternoons were spent by the pool, reading, napping, or playing board games. Other times, we would take a drive to nowhere, or maybe take a picnic to the mountains with family or friends. Sometimes we drove up to the lake and lazed around the beach or cast a line in the water to see what we could catch. These were cherished times.

As we age, these are the memories that fill the treasure chests of our minds. Have you wondered what today's children will remember about Sundays? Will their treasure chests be filled with Mom doing household chores or Dad working in solitude, finishing up last week's work?

Just as the rain refreshes the earth, restful Sundays refresh our souls. We desperately need to focus on restructuring our lives to allow for rest and relaxation. Without rest, we will run out of gas, emotionally, physically, and spiritually. God did not institute a cram fest. Instead, He set aside a day of rest because He knew we needed it. After all, even God rested on the seventh day. How about you? Try it for four weeks. Rest on the Sabbath. There's a good chance you will soon relish this gift from God.

Remember the Sabbath day by keeping it holy.
—Exodus 20:8 NIV

WHAT IF?

It was time for that yearly physical. It always seemed like a waste of time, but I knew it was important and that I felt good when the doctor pronounced me in good health. I sat fiddling with my phone while in the waiting room. I had been patient for forty-five minutes, and now my impatience was on the rise. Thank goodness for Kindle on the phone. It affords me the luxury of reading my book without lugging that three-pound, seven-hundred-page mammoth everywhere I go.

Ding! I had a text message. Now for that internal debate. Do I get out of Kindle to read the message or just ignore it? I decided to continue with my reading. Another fifteen minutes slipped by, and I had been waiting for an hour. I went to the little glass window, tapped it, and asked, "Do you think it will be much longer?"

A young girl with pink hair looked up from her computer and said, "You should be next. Hopefully, it won't be too long, but the doctor had an emergency, so we are running a little behind. Thank you for being so patient."

Well, that took the sting out of my prepared retort. Someone else needed the doctor worse than I, even if it meant waiting for who knows how long. But I would be next. I returned to my seat and picked up my reading. Ding! There it went again, another message, but I determined that I was not going to get tied up in a texting duel just when I was going to be next. Isn't that the worst? You answer a text, and that brings another and another, and you have to answer; otherwise the other person thinks you're mad or upset. More than a few minutes passed, and I was deeply engrossed in my book—so much so I didn't immediately recognize that my name was called. Ding! There it went again, and the nurse stood patiently at the door, while I closed my Kindle and gathered my bag.

I survived the inevitable weight, height, blood pressure, and temperature protocol. In the middle of the "What brought you in today?" question-and-answer session came another ding. There it went again. In my frustration, I shut off my phone. I simply could not be bothered. Not now!

Again, another wait—the doctor wait. I have to admit my patience was wearing thin, and my agitation was hitting a new high. It had now been nearly two hours, and again, here I was waiting. Wasn't my time worth anything? My mind swirled with thoughts of what I could have accomplished if only ...

The doctor came in. He apologized for taking up so much of my time, but someone else had had a medical crisis. The doctor examined me and declared I was healthy. All was well with me, and after about fifteen minutes, I was on my way home.

After I got home, I got busy fixing supper, reading the mail, and tidying up. I completely forgot my phone. After supper, I remembered and picked up my phone only to discover I had seven messages. When I opened the text page, I saw they were all from the same person. I didn't recognize the number because it was not a regular phone number. It was one of those funny five-number ones; it was from 77-7777. I opened the first message, and it read:

Call to Me and I will answer you ...

I opened the next message and it read:

... and tell you great and unsearchable things

And another:

... you do not know ...

The next one read:

Shouldn't you have mercy on your fellow servant ...

It was followed by:

Just as I had mercy on you?

Next:

Give as freely as you have received.

At this point, the hair was standing up on my arms, and my heart was beating like a jackhammer. Who sent these to me? I returned to the first message. *Call to me and I will answer you.* Yes, I had been a bit lax in my prayer life. *And tell you great and unsearchable things.* What a promise. *You do not know.* That is so true, I certainly don't know it all.

The next message struck me like a lightning bolt: *Shouldn't you have mercy on your fellow servant ... Just as I had mercy on you?* It was then I recalled my frustration and agitation at being left sitting for so long to see the doctor while he was attending some poor soul who was in distress. How could I have been so self-absorbed?

The last message—well, it challenged me. *Give as freely as you have received.*

Did this happen like I just said? No. But upon reflection, they were words that were part of my random thoughts as I stewed and fretted in the waiting room. I often wonder what else He has said to me that I didn't hear. Do I truly listen for His Word? A "ding" would be nice to get my attention, but even that didn't work because I was determined to do something other than read the text. Wouldn't it be awful if He didn't listen to us when we prayed? We expect Him to be available to us anytime we pray. Likewise, we should be prepared to hear Him when He whispers to us.

Call to me and I will answer, and tell you [and even show you] great and mighty things,] which have been confined and hidden], which you do not know and understand and cannot distinguish.
—Jeremiah 33:3 AMP

THE SILENT WITNESS

There is a popular feature on a local television station called *Silent Witness*, where people call in anonymously if they have witnessed or have information about a crime. One night while watching this segment, I thought about how much more carefully we might choose our words and actions if we knew there was a silent witness observing our behaviors. For example, consider the following.

It was Saturday morning, and Brian bounded from bed. Excited, he quickly showered and brushed his teeth and slipped into his clothes. Last week, his father had promised to take him to see the Blue Angels, the navy's precision flying team. He hurried down the hall and paused outside of his parents' bedroom. Tentatively, he knocked and quietly called, "Dad. Dad. It's Saturday." No response. He tried again. "Dad, Dad, we have to go early."

From behind the door, he heard his father stir. "Uh ... Brian, it's barely daylight. Go back to bed."

"But, Dad, the Blue Angels ..."

"I said go back to bed or watch TV or something. Just leave me alone."

Disappointed, Brian returned to the living room, where he sat waiting. Nearly an hour passed before his father finally arose. Brian jumped and ran down the hall. "Dad, can we go now?"

"Go where?" his father asked.

"To see the Blue Angels. You promised."

"Oh, yeah. Look, Brian, I'm sorry, but I'm just too tired. I worked all week, and I just want to stay home and chill today. Sorry, pal. Maybe next time. Okay?"

Brian turned so his father could not see the tears that welled in his eyes. It was always the same. He had just hoped this time it would be different.

Maybe Dad was too tired, or maybe he didn't want to go, but he forgot that his promise was a vow to his son. Sometimes we think of vows as only those things we do in a formal ceremony, such as a wedding or ordination. But all promises, regardless of size, are vows. By being untrue to our vows, we will hurt and cause distress to someone. If we cannot be found faithful in the smaller promises, then how can we be entrusted to be faithful in larger ones?

Unfortunately, many times promises are made in the flurry of the moment, with good intentions and without consideration of long-term consequence. Our failure to keep our promise snowballs to making excuses and sometimes outright lying to cover our blunders. Brian is learning to distrust his elders, and distrust leads to disrespect. He is learning that keeping his word is more an issue of rationalization than an issue of character and developing trust.

The old adage "if you can't say something nice, don't say anything at all" could easily be restated. "If you can't keep the promise, don't make it."

Every time we make a promise, there is a silent witness. One who knows our every action and thought and hears everything that proceeds from our mouth. Nearly every day, we make a promise of some sort. Sometimes, we make more than we realize. It might be a good family exercise to have each member jot down each promise they make and then post them on your refrigerator as a reminder that God is a silent witness to all that is said and done. Where would we stand if our lives were the subject of a television broadcast and God called in as the silent witness?

But let your statement be 'yes, yes' or 'no, no'—anything beyond these is evil.
—Matthew 5:37 NASB

A Defining Moment

My granddaughters love to come to the country. From the moment they arrive, they are totally immersed in outside activities. They are either racing around the barn, climbing a fence, drawing pictures in the dirt, making mud pies, helping feed the animals, grooming horses, or going on a trail ride. Television and video games are unimportant and all but forgotten. They willingly go to bed at night, exhausted from the day of play and fresh air.

One Saturday morning, they eagerly arose before dawn. We sat together and watched the sun rise over the mountains and gazed at the beautiful silhouettes of the sentinels of the desert, the saguaro cacti. Then one of the girls said, "Wow, Nana, that's so pretty. In the city, it just gets light outside in the morning." At this point, I wondered if she had ever seen a sunrise or if this sunrise would be a defining moment in her life—much as it was in mine more than sixty years ago.

When I was ten, I spent my entire summer vacation with my aunt Ethel and uncle Ed. They had a small farm in Indiana, complete with chickens, cows, pigs, a big bull named Bill, a truck garden, hand-pumped well, and a fully operational outhouse. I arrived there as a sheltered, indulged, pampered, prissy city girl and left the country a loving tomboy. A case of reverse metamorphosis occurred that summer; a butterfly changed into a caterpillar and learned that life as a caterpillar is pretty good.

I stepped from the car with my suitcase, patent leather shoes, frilly socks, neatly pressed dress, and perfectly coifed curls. Aunt Ethel, a feisty little woman of boundless energy and a wicked sense of humor, took one look at me and shook her head and sighed. Later, as she helped me unpack, she asked, "Don't you have any sensible clothes?" Not waiting for an answer, she grabbed some feed sacks she had washed and saved, sat down at her treadle sewing machine, and whipped out a simple pullover shirts and some drawstring shorts. She found a pair of old goulashes for me to wear until we could go into town and by some sensible shoes. Those flour-sack shorts and shirts were the softest and most comfortable things I ever wore. I soon learned about the convenience of those shorts when I asked where the bathroom was and was ushered down the well-worn path to the outhouse. And I discovered that night a "slop jar" beneath my bed for inside nighttime use.

I learned that water was pumped and carried to the house and that the best food ever prepared by a human being came from a wood-burning cookstove. I found out that it was possible to take a bath in the kitchen in a big washtub.

Another of life's lesson was taught when I was sent to the house because a cow in the barnyard was about to calve. Secretly, I witnessed the miracle of birth by peeping through the curtains.

Aunt Ethel showed me how to slide my hand beneath a hen to collect the eggs and how to grab an unruly rooster. With fascination, I watched the barn cats race to the milk house for offerings of warm milk froth. I learned how to hoe and harvest a garden. I learned to can vegetables for winter, a chore I still love to this day.

In the evenings, tales of *The Shadow, Fibber Magee and Molly, Amos and Andy,* and *The Southern Indiana Farm Report* played on the radio. Aunt Ethel did the mending and taught me how to embroider. My first project was to embroider designs on flour-sack dish towels. She promised if I got good enough, she'd let me do some pillowcases for my hope chest, whatever that was. For the first time in my life, I got really dirty and saw the sun rise.

Perhaps I have romanticized my memories of farm life, but there is no doubt that summer was a defining moment in my life. You see, under Aunt Ethel and Uncle Ed's tutelage, I learned about God, how to love all of His creatures, how to appreciate His handiwork in nature, and I saw His bountiful providence.

Hopefully, in the future, my granddaughters will recall their first desert sunrise. If, each morning, we removed our lenses of cynicism, stress, and frustration and put on God's glasses of wonderment, we, too, could see His majesty and His providence and recognize His love for us. Just a few moments of meditation at dawn can fill your heart with peace as you see God's reflected glory at sunrise.

Whoever is wise, let him understand these things,
Whoever is discerning, let him
understand and know them;
For the ways of the Lord are right,
And the righteous will walk in them, but
transgressors stumble in them.
—Hosea 14:9 NASB

Looking for Help in All the Wrong Places

While driving home the other night, I was listening to talk radio. On this particular evening, the host had a famous psychic guest who was taking calls from listeners seeking advice on a variety of issues. I have heard psychics on the radio before, and usually their predictions are so general that the revelations could fit a variety of situations. This man was different. He spoke with such authority, and his responses were more direct than most. On this evening, his advice was given freely. If, however, you wanted a more in-depth response, you would need to visit his website or call his 800 number with credit card in hand.

A grieving widow called and wanted to know if her deceased husband was still present in spirit, because she thought she felt his presence. His answer thoroughly angered me.

He told here unequivocally that her deceased husband's spirit was indeed near her and that his spirit was still earthbound and had not passed on to the afterlife because she, obviously, still needed him. Further, he told her that if she wished to communicate with him, she should do so as she drifted toward sleep. This was the time when his spirit would visit, and he would respond to her in her dreams.

Next, a man called in and asked about a marital problem, which he disclosed on the air. This genie of the airways immediately answered that call. His response was that the man should expect resolution in October.

Another person called, wanting to know if he should leave his job of five years. This mastermind of prediction told him that he should leave his job because there was a great opportunity on the immediate horizon but that it would only be available if he showed his willingness to take a risk. After displaying this magnificent piece of wisdom, he asked the man what he did for a living. Really? Shouldn't he have known the man's occupation?

Finally, the call that was most tragic was from a single mom who simply asked, "What's in my future? Will my financial situation improve?" The swami had the audacity to tell this young woman that it was very likely she would win a lot of money from the lottery if she played consistently for twelve straight days. This was her future. If the woman was having a difficult situation, why would he ask her to risk what little resources she might have by playing the lottery?

More calls flooded in. For the most part, these were desperate people with real problems. They were looking for *hope*. They were grasping for *strength*. They needed *assurance*. This charlatan was toying with their emotions. He was giving out his foolishness in hopes of making more money. Unfortunately, they were looking for help in all the wrong places.

Many people earnestly believe in psychics, mediums, and psychic intuition. Usually, they are drawn into the deceitful and satanic web of the psychic experience out of fear of the unknown, or lack of understanding of their circumstances, or unusual events. What I find difficult to rationalize is why not look to the Creator for an explanation rather to a self-promoted charlatan? The idea of paying for someone to help you find hope, strength, and assurance is truly ludicrous when it is offered to all who seek it for free.

Another area of psychic phenomena that intrigues practically everyone is the desire to have insight into future events. This is evidenced by all of the predictions for the future that blast across the tabloids and magazine covers ever January. Driven by fear or curiosity, millions of dollars are spent on magazines and books in hope of gleaning a look into the future. Astrology is another such minefield. Again, why read the tabloids and magazines when the greatest book ever written, the Word of God, gives a precise and detailed picture of the world to come? From His Word, we can glimpse into life hereafter. We can follow world events and see God's plan for humankind unfolding. And it truly becomes a road map for life.

The major differences between those who seek out psychics and those who follow the Bible are the demands placed upon the believer or follower. A psychic will make you feel good for the moment. The Bible teaches moral imperatives. The believer learns that by living according to biblical standards, they have hope. They grow in strength and receive everlasting assurance. When problems arise or our curiosity is piqued, let us look for help in all the right places—in the pages of His Word.

And God is able to make all grace abound to you
so that always having all sufficiency in everything
you may have an abundance for every good deed;
—2 Corinthians 9:8 NASB

WHEN GOD IS SILENT

My son is a technocratic wizard. He is always the first to have all the new gadgets, software programs, and equipment. He constantly teases me about how resistant to change and technologically challenged I am. While there may be some merit in his comments, I do not consider them to be entirely accurate. After all, I use a computer daily, write and send emails, order items online, check out Facebook, use my microwave, enjoy CDs on my stereo, listen to Pandora through my phone or other Bluetooth devices (although Amazon Fire and Sling are still a somewhat of a mystery), sew on a computerized sewing machine (although I prefer my sixty-six-year-old Singer Featherweight machine), and use those infernal, impersonal ATM machines.

Speaking of ATMs, recently, when I attempted to make a deposit, I was unable to complete the transaction due to a damaged strip on my card. The same day, my husband had a similar experience when he tried to withdraw cash from an ATM. He had forgotten to remove the expired card from his wallet. Of course, there are many other reasons why this technological marvel might refuse to comply with our requests. For whatever reason, they fail. The experience is disconcerting until we figure out what caused the mighty ATM to fall silent.

In today's frenetic world, sometimes we look for the same convenience and expediency in our spiritual life. We treat God as if he was the big ATM in the sky. We offer our prayer cards and expect that He will be forthcoming to meet our every request. When He doesn't pour forth the expected blessings or fails to answer our prayers, we often become frustrated or even angry with Him rather than looking for the cause of His silence.

Our prayer card may be damaged with unrepentant and unconfessed sin. Or perhaps we have failed to make regular deposits of praise and thanksgiving for blessings received. Maybe we have broken fellowship or moved away from Him, and our card is on inactive status.

If we are neglectful in balancing our bank records, we are sure to run into problems. Likewise, if we neglect our spiritual life, we will face difficulties. God's silence definitely gets our attention.

So, how do we cope with His silence? First, we need to recognize that God is not impersonal, nor is He a convenient push-button God. We must admit that there is a problem, and then His silence is a positive rather than a negative. Second, we need to slow down and consider our balance sheet. Take a look at your debits versus your credits. How does the balance sheet read? I wonder what would happen if we opened our Bible as often as we open our checkbooks or use our debit cards.

God's silence may encourage us to grow, or it may be the instrument of His discipline that forces us to search our hearts and examine our faith. While His silence is disconcerting, we know that He answers every prayer, though in His time and not in ours.

It has been said that silence is golden, and nowhere are these words truer than when God is silent. Sometimes it is years before we can look through the glasses of hindsight and discover that what appeared to be unanswered prayer was, in fact, a perfectly answered prayer.

Finally, we need to deal with any deficit by depositing more time in prayer, Bible study, and praise. We need to reactivate our cards and seek His forgiveness to cleanse a damaged strip.

Of one thing we can be assured. His silence is never the result of insufficient funds. The bank of His love is overflowing, and we can always draw on the funds of His love. Even in silence, He is nearby, waiting for us to call upon and draw closer to Him.

"You shall not put the Lord your God to the test."
—Matthew 4:7 NASB

LIVING THE DREAM

In the mideighties, we moved to paradise—Honolulu, Hawaii—where the weather is perfect, there are rainbows nearly every day, and the people are warm and welcoming. My husband had always been enthralled with the movie *South Pacific* and the fantastic character of Bloody Mary. Yes, this was definitely on his bucket list, although I don't think he met Bloody Mary.

What can one say about the beautiful, refreshing ocean and white beaches? Spectacular! It was warm and humid, but we were kept comfortable with the blowing trade winds. One of the more interesting experiences occurred when we rented our first condo. I went looking for the thermostat for the air-conditioning and furnace. There was none. Why? Because there was no need. Just open or close your windows to get the temperature you desire. Being close to the equator, the temperatures were fairly constant, winter to summer—just a few degrees difference. Yet, comically, as islanders, we wore sweaters and coats during winter months, just because of the calendar. We always knew who actually lived there and who did not. The tourists wore summer clothes and sandals with socks. They took pictures of everything, even street signs. We often hiked Diamondhead, which was just down the street from where we lived. We also loved hiking upon near the

Pali Highway and going back through the thick jumble of exotic plants and flowers. Other weekends, we would find a festival with beautiful music, Hawaiian dancing, sweet-smelling flowers, and food vendors who produced the most wonderful food for takeout. Or, the alternative, we would just find a quiet spot on a less-known beach. Yes, we were in paradise.

However, it wasn't long before the reality of actually living in Hawaii as opposed to simply visiting became apparent. Hawaii was in the midst of a housing sell-off to foreign investors who were purchasing property at overinflated prices, causing the cost of housing to skyrocket. The next big shock came at the grocery store. At that time, Oahu had no discount merchandisers such as Walmart, Kmart, or Costco. Grocery stores were locally owned—again, no Kroger, Safeway, Ralphs, Vons, or Albertsons. Milk was well over five dollars per gallon, and pineapples were more expensive than on the mainland. Add to that, so was sugar. There are no longer any refineries for sugar in Hawaii, thus, even though it was grown in Hawaii, it was shipped to the mainland to be refined and then shipped back to Hawaii. Nearly everything in Hawaii is imported, including nearly dead Christmas trees. By the time they arrive, needles are falling off, and the trees are pretty pathetic and costly.

On the upside, all one needed to be outfitted to live in Hawaii was a swimsuit, shorts, tops, flip-flops (slippers), and a couple of muumuus. With this wardrobe, you were set for any occasion. But we were living the dream. Nothing else mattered.

Hawaiian time is a real phenomenon. Time is only a suggestion when it comes to hanging with friends. Three o'clock can mean two thirty, three thirty, or four o'clock. This relaxed attitude causes less stress but can be a bit disconcerting to a newcomer. Another fun thing is that you take your shoes off outside the front door before you enter the house. This is expected. Even the police or repairman slip off their shoes before entering your home. As you walk through a neighborhood, a party is easy to spot based on the number of slippers (flip-flops) and shoes outside the front door. Like so many other traditions, there are several versions as to why, but the tradition of taking off your slippers before entering a house comes down to one of respect. It does help in keeping down germs, dust, and sand from tracking up your floors.

As I reflect on our time in Hawaii, it is with great fondness except for an overshadowing failure. God clearly showed me that we were in love with the lifestyle of paradise regardless of the costs. We quickly took for granted all the blessings of living in an earthly paradise. We spent many more Sundays at the beach, hiking, or going to festivals than we did in church. I remember we were amazed at how skimpily churches were attended there. It was (at that time) truly a field white unto harvest. Rather than getting involved in church and doing what we knew we should, we chose to relax and enjoy ourselves. (I bet we all have heard that explanation for not going to church.) We did join a church, but we were not steady in attending or giving. There were so many opportunities opened for us. But we ignored His call and fell far short by our putting love of nature, beach, festivals, and hikes above our love for the Lord. This is hard to say, but I am ashamed to admit we were guilty of idolatry. So, during our nearly ten years there, we followed the easy path of secular pleasures rather than the narrow road of faithfulness.

Our life in Hawaii was like a river. It flowed by, and that time can never be recovered. Now, life continues to flow. It is hard to believe that we could be so easily swayed, that we put aside the Lord with so little thought. Yes, we failed miserably to walk on the path He laid out before us. Paradise is not only beautiful but enticing and deceptive. It is truly very empty without Him.

The only redeeming factor is His forgiveness and that we no longer take our walk with Him for granted. We seek to serve Him wherever He leads. Thank you, Lord, for your patience with us. Thank you for removing the scales from our eyes. And thank you for the blessings you afforded us when we least deserved them. Thank you for your forgiveness and grace.

But avoid worldly and empty chatter, for
it will lead to further ungodliness.
—2 Timothy 2:16 NASB

A Vacation That Keeps on Giving

Several years ago, my husband and I had the privilege of going on a vacation to the Holy Land, Israel. Prior to this trip, I often thought it would be nice to visit the land with such rich history and to walk in places where Jesus walked.

We had heard about the trip through our church and were excited about the fact that Dr. David Reagan was leading the trip. His ministry is devoted to study of prophecy, and he had been there more than thirty times with groups from various churches. We rightly figured that he would know where to go and make sure we got to see the most important sites. For months after we signed up, we read everything we could about modern-day Israel and, of course, checked out things in the Bible.

From the very start, this was the ideal trip. Planes were on time, not overcrowded, and we had smooth flights. We crossed the Atlantic at night, and the first sight we beheld at daybreak was the sun rising over the Mediterranean Sea, with a glimpse of the boot heel of Italy. This is not a travelogue inasmuch as recalling every stop along the way. I can do that, as it is burnt in my memory bank, and I hope I never lose it. It is more a tale of how profoundly this trip affected me.

Suffice it to say, the entire itinerary and the weather were magnificent. What we took away from the trip was immeasurable. Truly the Word of God came alive. No longer did we imagine those special places. The Israeli people are warm, pleasant, friendly, and ever so helpful. The religious sites touched our souls, and the secular ones brought us to an understanding of the current state of Israel and the Jewish people's drive to regain and hold their homeland.

It is shocking today to read and hear on television the obtuse reasoning of some who want Israel to be either eradicated or forced to return lands to a people who basically have no roots or familial interest in the lands of Israel. The biggest challenge seems to be to provide proof of this being the Israeli homeland from centuries ago. In December 2016, at the Ophel excavation site, the seal of King Hezekiah was discovered. He reined in Jerusalem for twenty-nine years. There is an inscription that clearly states, "Belonging to Hezekiah (son of) Ahaz king of Judah." This was later dated to be 704 BCE. There are many things that show this land is the Promised Land of the Bible, given by the highest authority, God, to the Jewish people. Never, at any time since the children of Israel entered this land, was this land not inhabited by the Jewish people. A few always remained.

The trip afforded us the opportunity to be ceremonially baptized in the Jordan River. This was an experience that sank deep into my soul. The memories are as vivid today as they were when we were there. A few other experiences follow: taking a ride on a fisherman's boat on the Sea of Galilee; from the Tel of Megiddo, looking down upon the Valley of Jezreel (plains of Armageddon); swimming in the Dead Sea; going to the top of Masada; visiting Christ's birthplace in Bethlehem; looking at the sealed gate in Jerusalem from the Mount of Olives; singing in the Garden of Gethsemane; reflecting upon His last moments in the Upper Room; walking the Via Delorosa in the crown jewel, Jerusalem; and enjoying the moments of resurrection at the empty tomb. Finally, but not last by any means, was a most memorable event, visiting the Holocaust Museum and the various displays of humanity's inhumanity.

Truly, this is the vacation that keeps on giving. As I read the Bible now, visions of the places we visited come flooding into my mind. Yes, the Living Word is alive, filled with history, love, hope, faith, and our future. Yes, what started as a vacation turned into a pilgrimage. A trip to the Holy Land will benefit anyone, from believer to atheist. You will feel the soul of the Hebrew people of old and the resurgence of the spirit of the Jews of today.

For the word of God is living and active, sharper
than any two-edged sword, piercing to the division
of soul and spirit, of joints and marrow, and
discerning the thoughts and intentions of the heart.
—2 Timothy 4:12 ESV

THE RED-CARPET
SYNDROME

During the winter season each year, we get a dose of the red-carpet syndrome. You know all of those award shows: *The Grammys, The Golden Globes, The Oscars, The CMAs, The Emmys,* and so on. I suppose it is because people are trapped in their homes due to foul weather. Each year, it seems like they add another award show. At the heart of each show is the infamous stroll on the red carpet. Stroll is the appropriate word because the celebrities take a step or two and then pause for photographs, then take another step or two and answer the infamous question, "Who are you wearing?" They take a few more steps and sidle up to their favorite television programs like *TMZ* or *Inside Edition*. Oh yes, it is quite the event with all of that talking, posing, sighing, and strutting.

They borrow or negotiate for gowns or tuxedos from famous designers, wear expensive jewels on loan, and utter profound words of hired writers. It is a spectacle to behold and a narcissist's dream. Are we suffering from the red-carpet syndrome? Millions of people hang on their every word, ooh and ah over the clothes, and wait patiently to catch a glimpse of their favorite singer, comedian, actor, or actress. Many of these celebrities are truly talented and creative, and if they choose to honor one another's accomplishments, that is fine.

It becomes a problem when they believe their own hype and become convinced that the people (a.k.a. as the little people) want or need to see them and hear what they have to say. Do *you* really care who won an award for cinemaphotography or who was on the team of wardrobe designers? Or what they had to say when accepting their award? Really, do you care? Do you want a political diatribe from people who make a living pretending to be someone other than themselves? Sure, they have opinions, but don't you have opinions just as important, without a soapbox upon which you can expound? Thus, why is what they have to say any more important? If the truth be known, this exhibition of self-aggrandizement will follow the trail of two sins—the love of self and money. Seriously, have we returned to the days of Rome?

The larger issue is to what degree do we, as a society, elevate entertainers to the status of idols? Our mere interest fuels these shows and, in turn, feeds the egos of the entertainers. We can appreciate their talent without making them idols. So what is the definition of idolatry? The *Cambridge Dictionary* defines idolatry as "great admiration for someone, often too great." It is the veneration of someone or something other than God.

If we suffer from the red-carpet syndrome, we are guilty of idol worship and, by our actions of adulation, encourage others to do likewise. We, too, become more and more self-centered and lustful for the same money and power shown by those we desire to emulate. But there is hope. In recent years, the viewership of such programs has slipped significantly. May we recognize the power of the Lord, the salvation through Jesus, and the internal workings of the Holy Spirt. May we worship God only, as He is the only one who deserves such veneration, praise, and glory.

Therefore, my beloved, flee from idolatry.
—1 Corinthians 10:14 ESV

CHRISTMAS AT AUNT MAGGIE'S

During the holidays, almost anything can trigger memories of Christmases past. Recently, while crocheting an afghan, my mind wandered to a special Christmas memory. My dad's family was small, but not lacking for interesting characters. One such relative was his only aunt, Aunt Maggie. One year, much to my parents' chagrin, she insisted on hosting the family Christmas celebration.

An unconventional woman by the 1960s standards, she was outspoken and a little brazen. Mother even said she was a bit bawdy. In her late eighties and widowed for nearly forty years, she was totally self-sufficient and fiercely independent. Each year, she made her pilgrimage to Florida in her Nash Rambler and annually received one or two speeding citations along the way. She preferred a frosty bottle of beer to iced tea. She loved doing crafts and didn't care much for housework and cooking. Every time we visited Aunt Maggie's home, Mother spent a lot of time whispering to Dad and rolling her eyes heavenward. For Aunt Maggie, life was simply one adventure after another.

She was a stooped woman with white, mussed hair whose fashion tastes never graduated beyond print housedresses and orthopedic shoes. As she grew older, she became a real touchy-feely person. She liked to rub her hands across your face, pull on your ears, grasp your hand, and lead you to wherever she deigned that you should sit.

A type of orderly disorder reigned in Aunt Maggie's home. She had crocheted doilies everywhere: on the back of davenport (couch for those who don't remember davenports), on the arms of chairs, on tables, and under lamps. The hassock was piled high with bright afghans. Normally, the dining table with its beautiful crocheted tablecloth was all but hidden by her latest craft projects. The beds were covered with quilts, not one but two or three. Atop the beds were lots of dolls wearing elaborately crocheted gowns. The remaining flat space was covered with handmade knickknacks. On her dressing table lay her prized possession, a hand mirror encrusted with seashells.

On this Christmas day, she met us on the porch wearing a crocheted poinsettia corsage pinned to her blue dress. As she led Mother into the house, Dad smiled at me and pointed to Aunt Maggie's feet. She wore a pair of mismatched crocheted house slippers. One was blue and white, and the other was red and yellow.

An unusual Christmas tree sat in the middle of the dining table. This crocheted and stiffly starched contraption slid over a wine bottle and was decorated with painted bottle caps and a string of small seashells. The table was set with mixed-matched plates, glasses, and flatware. On each chair lay a package wrapped in plain brown paper and tied with brightly colored yarn.

Mother's nose told her something was amiss in the kitchen. Sure enough, the corn was scorched. She helped Aunt Maggie bring the dinner to the table. After the prayer, Aunt Maggie told us we couldn't eat until we opened our presents. I received a pair of purple and red crocheted house slippers; Mother got and orange dresser doily; Dad's gift was a green and yellow crocheted necktie. Aunt Maggie giggled with glee as we oohed and ahhed over our gifts. Christmas dinner was cold and not too good. The ham was dry, the corn was burnt, the sweet potatoes were hard, and the lopsided latticework pie tops were slightly underbaked.

After dinner, Aunt Maggie rummaged through a bag and brought out skeins of yarn and crochet needles. She asked if I wanted to learn how to crochet. I soon mastered the chain stitch, and in the next couple of hours, she patiently showed me other stitches. She took my piece and felt along the nubby rows and told me where my stitches were too tight or where I missed a loop. Then she unraveled it, and we started over. While her hands flew up and down the rows, she reminisced and told of escapades at the St. Louis World Fair. She regaled us with hair-raising tales of her solitary travels out west in the 1920s and '30s. Years later, I wondered if she might have been the infamous Bonnie of Bonnie and Clyde. All too quickly, afternoon turned to evening, and soon it was time to go. She grabbed our arms and walked us to the door. There she hugged us tightly and kissed us goodbye. Seven days later on New Year's Eve, the Lord took Aunt Maggie home. At her wake, the funeral home was packed with people. My parents were surprised that she had so many friends. Many of the mourners were nurses from a local hospital. One nurse told of how Aunt Maggie had made hundreds of pairs of slippers and lap robes for patients. Another told of the many sock monkeys she had made for the children's ward. Then Aunt Maggie's doctor told of how, despite her near blindness, she continued to crochet beautiful floral bouquets for the patient rooms.

Blindness? What blindness? It was then we learned of Aunt Maggie's battle with diabetes, how over the past couple of years her eyesight had been failing rapidly and that she was technically blind. What a shock! Why didn't we know? Were we really that unobservant? Or were we too preoccupied with her eccentricities? Perhaps we were just too self-absorbed to really notice or care.

How could we have missed something so obvious? The signs were there, but we failed to see them—the overcooked ham, the burned corn, the crazy pie tops, her two different slippers, her touchy-feely actions, and her color selection for our gifts.

Years later, after my father passed away, I found that yellow and green tie hung prominently on his tie rack. Mother told me that Aunt

Maggie's Christmas tie was a daily reminder to be vigilant, observant, and sensitive to the plight of others.

Just as there were obvious signs pointing to Aunt Maggie's blindness, on that first Christmas there were obvious signs pointing to the birth of Christ. But now as then, some people heed the signs and follow through, while other fail to see and falter.

For a child is born, to us, a son is given; And the government shall be upon His shoulder, and His name shall be called, Wonderful Counselor, Mighty God, Everlasting Father, Prince of Peace.
—Isaiah 9:6 ESV

REAL WEALTH

A few weeks ago, I was having lunch with a friend when she dropped a bombshell. She and her husband of thirty-eight years were separating. Apparently, her husband came home and announced that he could no longer live a lie, and with that, he stated he wanted a divorce. Adding insult to injury, he told her he had wanted out of the marriage for the past twenty years and that he hadn't really loved her for most of the marriage. Incredulous, she asked him why he hadn't said anything before now. He said, "Oh, I don't know. I just always thought things would get better—if I worked hard enough, we'd have a good life. Now, all I have is a lot of stuff and nothing else."

It was true. From all outward appearances, they lived a charmed life. They have two healthy, college-educated children, a beautifully furnished home, two new cars, a houseboat, membership in the country club, a summer condo in San Diego, success in their careers, minimal debt, a large 401(k), and a stock portfolio with retirement plans all set in place. And the list of goodies goes on and on.

I asked her if she had seen any evidence of his discontent. She replied, "Oh, I suppose the signs were there, but I didn't pick up on them. He was always preoccupied with his newest hobby. He loved everything from jet skiing to model trains. You've seen all of his phases. You know, from coin collecting to sports memorabilia. He was always collecting something. He told me that he loved me, so I just went along for the ride. I tried to be interested in his various pursuits. For heaven's sake, I started jogging with him, even though my arthritic knees nearly buckled."

I repeated my question, "So, you saw nothing that would lead you to believe he was unhappy?" Sadly, she shook her head no. I was at a loss as to how to console her. In a moment, her whole adult life had been fractured, and she didn't know why. I asked her if she had been happy all these years. She sadly shook her head no.

"I always knew something was missing. I couldn't put my finger on it, but something was missing. Anytime I started to think about it, he seemed to know and would surprise me with a weekend getaway or buy me something special. He's great at that, you know. But I guess he's right; all we have now is a bunch of stuff."

When I got home, I was looking for something that I could write in a card that might help her, so I pulled out one of Mother's old diaries. Mother started each day reading her Bible and writing in her diary. What words of wisdom are contained in these battered old spiral notebooks! At the top of the page, she'd jot down a thought for the day. I think she copied them from the newspaper, books, or sermon notes, but on this very day fifty years before, her diary entry was to the point: "Contentment makes the poor man rich and discontent makes a rich man poor."

While those were not appropriate words to share with my friend at that point in time, it gave me pause to reflect on the importance of contentment in marriage. I couldn't help but wonder how many marriages have suffered and been broken because the parties never understood that the principle of being content is one of the foundation stones of marriage. Our wedding vows imply that we should be content in richer and poorer, in sickness and health. All too often, couples fail to recognize that being content is a state of mind. It is not a collection of things, children, or the absence of obstacles. It takes work to grab hold of the moment and find joy in the little things in good times and in bad. When young couples get married, we always wish them much happiness. What we really should wish for them is daily contentment. No one has ever found happiness in a state of discontent. Yes, real wealth comes to those who are content, regardless of their things or the balance in their checkbook.

Not that I speak from want, for I have learned to
be content in whatever circumstances I am.
—Philippians 4:11 NASB

SHELTER OR STORMY SLOPE

The law firm where I worked moved into new office space. As office administrator, some of my tasks were to oversee the decorating (with partner supervision, of course) and keep things moving expeditiously. After much discussion, review of office furniture brochures, and visits to local stores, it was determined that a few senior partners needed new desk systems specifically constructed to meet their individual needs. Translated: they wanted custom-built desks.

Little did I know that this would be neither an economical nor efficient process. In fact, it would take nearly three years for the desks to be delivered and installed. Over the course of four months, several cabinet-furniture carpenters from, literally, around the world were interviewed. At last, one was selected.

First were the meetings where the partners discussed with the carpenter what they wanted in a desk system. Then there were numerous measuring appointments. Next came the conferences to go over preliminary designs, and finally, it took twelve meetings to review and revise the final drawings. Finally, everyone gathered to sign off on the plans and execute the carpenter's contract. Keep in mind that these were only the formal meetings. There were an untold number of luncheons, golf course get-togethers, and phone conferences. It has been said that if Moses was a committee, the children of Israel would have never gotten out of Egypt. The same might be said for lawyers.

After the flurry of meetings, several months passed. It seemed that everyone forgot about the desks, including the carpenter. I understood that on one desk there was a problem in securing the perfect piece of marble with the right shading and amount of veining from an Italian quarry. Beyond that hitch, I couldn't imagine what was taking so long. I called the carpenter's office several times, only to be told that he was out of the country. Now that was a bit disconcerting.

Eventually, he returned my call and seem a bit surprised when I asked him for a delivery date. He said it would be at least eighteen months and maybe twenty-four. Flabbergasted, I gasped aloud—so much so he felt obliged to enlighten me. In great detail, he told me what he had been doing over the many months since we last heard from him. The story was nearly as fascinating as were stories told by another carpenter two thousand years ago.

The desks were to be constructed from different woods. One partner had selected koa wood, while the other selected Philippine mahogany. Another chose Brazilian rosewood, and the fourth elected cherrywood.

The carpenter told of how he personally selected the trees from which the lumber would be milled to make the desk. This meant that he traveled around the world to find a forest of superior trees. Then he hiked into the forest, and his quest usually led him to a hillside or mountain slopes where the trees were most often battered by the storms.

Again, my curiosity was piqued. I asked, "Why?"

Patiently, he told me that trees on a stormy slope have deeper roots, and their cell structure is more compact, thus producing a finer grain to the lumber. He had been traveling, selecting trees, purchasing them, and arranging to have them chopped down, milled, and shipped—a very lengthy process in and of itself.

I rubbed my hand across my oak desk and looked at the grain. I was both intrigued and fascinated by how relevant the story of the trees is to our own lives. We spend so much time trying to get into that sheltered valley that we fail to recognize the blessings of living upon the stormy slopes. I thought of how the winds and storms of my life drove my roots deeper into His Word and how my branches sought the sky in prayer. I recalled that the human-interest stories that captivate and inspire me are usually based upon lives that are rooted on the stormy slopes and are able to weather out the prevailing winds without being uprooted.

As I recalled this story and sat to write it, thoughts kept reoccurring. So, with your indulgence and in tribute, I would like to say two of my daughters have faced many storms and some real hurricanes in their lives. But apparently their root structures go deep, and upon their faces shine the countenance of the Lord. The fine grain of their character reflects their love, perseverance, and humility. One was named Teacher of the Year, and the other is an extremely creative writer. Through them, I can clearly see the Carpenter at work.

For mothers everywhere, there is no greater sadness than to feel the chiseling and the abrasive sanding your child must endure. And there is no greater joy than to witness the polishing and see the fine grain of their character emerge.

"Refine them as silver is refined, and test them as gold is tested. They will call on My name, And I will listen and answer them; I will say, 'They are My people,' And they will say, 'The LORD is my God.'"
—Zechariah 13:9 NASB

DEADLINES

In the predawn hours of a Tuesday, I sat in my studio and picked up yet another demonstration piece that needed to be quilted by Saturday. As usual, I was under a deadline. Despite my best efforts, I apparently underestimated the time needed to finish this piece. My mind wandered with the rhythm of quilting. Obviously, the joy of doing the work diminished with the press of time. How did I get into these fixes?

For years, I have kept meticulous records on various projects as an aid to calculate actual time requirements to finish tasks on time. I purchased a computer program that projects working timelines. I check it frequently and try to follow it carefully.

I stopped and looked at my stitching. With speed, the stitches were getting longer. My head reeled with a repetitious chant of an old cliché, *Haste makes waste*. How nice it would be to finish an article or quilted piece in a day or two before the due date. To date, I haven't missed any deadlines, writing or quilting, but have put myself on a killer schedule in order to do so.

When I checked this project's timeline, I found that, in fact, I had allotted plenty of time to finish this quilt. I continued to flip forward, looking at more recent timelines, and found the source of my problem. I had added twenty-seven more tasks, all with earlier deadlines. Each day, I carved out little chunks of time to get those tasks completed and thus shortened the time allotted for my current project. Added to that, because I worked on the quilt daily, I deluded myself by believing the piece was nearer completion than it actually was.

At the heart of my problem is my inability to say no. Instead of reviewing my timelines before committing to another task, I usually just say, "Okay. I'll work it in." Sound familiar? When we agree to take on extra tasks, it is because we don't want to let someone down, we like to feel needed, perhaps it is an excuse because we really don't want work on the primary task, or we overestimate our abilities. In college, I learned to pull all-nighters when necessary, and when my children were small, I stayed up until the wee hours to get things accomplished. Physically, as we age, this is neither a good nor viable option.

The end result of this errant management strategy leads to unnecessary stress. My doctor repeatedly tells me that stress is the biggest threat to a person's health. It saps our strength, weakens our immune system, and, more importantly, robs us of the joy of life. Living by deadlines interferes with every facet of our daily life. Unfortunately, we put our personal time on hold. The benefits of quiet time are well documented and are invaluable to good mental, spiritual, and physical health.

Fifteen to thirty minutes spent in prayer, meditation, or study of God's Word is essential for a balanced life. It is here that we find encouragement, hope, direction, power, and true happiness. Seneca said, "One should count each day as a separate life." What a concept! If we looked at each day as an entire lifetime, how would our priorities change? Would we put ourselves under so much stress? Wouldn't we want to focus more on His creation, spend precious moments with family, pray that He would grant us a day (or life) filled with peace?

Coincidentally, in the book *Deadline*, Randy Alcorn wrote, "You wrote your life on earth." We do. We are the authors of our lives. We make the choices and set the priorities. While organization is important, no amount of record keeping or computer timelines can replace those precious moments spent communing with God. If we start each morning with Him, the rest of the day will fall into place. For when we write stress into everything we do, we just might meet a real *dead*line before it is due.

Delight yourself in the Lord and He will
give you the desires of your heart.
—Psalm 37:4 NASB

DON'T FORGET

Holidays great and small always lend themselves to reflection upon the history and traditions of that day. Why do we celebrate? Especially if it is a secular day. Such is the occasion of the Fourth of July. Historically, it is an important day, but do we go on celebrating it because it was the date of the signing of the Declaration of Independence? Or is there more to this day?

When Trivial Pursuit was the game rage, I thought it might be fun to develop a trivia game about Independence Day. While working on this project, I found out a lot of interesting things about July 4. These sidebars in history are often overlooked.

How about the fact that July 2, 1776, was truly our day of independence? It was on this day that the Continental Congress declared independence even as the British fleet and army arrived in New York.

Did you know that one of the greatest documents ever written, the Declaration of Independence, was actually a piece of propaganda intended to influence public opinion and gain support for the fledgling nation abroad?

As a writer, I appreciated the fact that it took Thomas Jefferson only a couple of days to draft the document. Further, it took the Continental Congress only four days to review, revise, and sign the

Declaration of Independence. I wonder if any other piece of legislation has ever been passed so expeditiously. Apparently, the members of that Congress cared more about the future of their country and less about political differences or ramifications.

John Adams, believing that the Declaration of Independence would be signed on July 2, prophesied that "this day" would be celebrated by generations to come with fireworks. He was off by a couple of days, but the prophecy of celebration with fireworks was right. The day has been continuously celebrated, but it wasn't until 1941 that the Fourth of July became a national holiday.

As British citizens, newly minted Americans knew they were committing an act of treason that would turn into a colonist rebellion and this country's first civil war. There were prominent families that remained loyal to the British, yet the revolutionaries were aware of the consequences such an act would have and were prepared to take responsibility for putting their names on this "traitorous document." They signed knowing full well that they faced death if captured. British Redcoats did capture, torture, and kill several signers. Many surviving signers lost their homes, families, landholdings, and businesses. Others faced even more tragedies during the Revolutionary War.

In 1826, as the fiftieth anniversary of the signing neared, Thomas Jefferson wrote, in what is believed to be one of his last letters, "For ourselves, let the annual return of this day forever refresh our recollections of these rights and an undiminished devotion to them." Interestingly, John Adams, the second president of the United States, and Thomas Jefferson, the third, both died within hours of each other on the fiftieth anniversary of the signing of the Declaration of Independence, July 4, 1826. The fifth president, James Monroe, died five years later on July 4, 1831. He was a signer to the Constitution and the last of the founding fathers.

At part of our future July 4 celebrations, it would be nice if we paused and gave thanks to our heavenly Father for guiding these patriots in their pursuit of freedom … our freedom. These courageous men literally put their lives on the line in doing so. They were men who were governed by a higher authority and acted upon His principles. They relied upon their faith in God. Every time we vote, we stand on their shoulders for the privilege they envisioned for us. Don't forget, it only took fifty-six men to change the course of history.

For lack of guidance a nation falls, but
victory is won through many advisors.
—Proverbs 11:14 NIV

OUR FATHER'S GIFT

For many years, I have looked at the paintings on my walls and recalled my father's passion for art. He was an aeronautical engineer by day and an artist by night. Born and raised in Indiana, he loved and painted the old covered bridges and barns that dotted the landscape of his youth. After moving to Arizona, he was captivated by all things southwestern. Before long, he was painting southwestern landscapes, still lifes, and Indian artifacts.

His early work reflected the preciseness of an engineer and was somewhat stilted. As the years passed, however, his style became flowing and free, and the canvases came alive. His paintings reflected a tranquility and peacefulness that held great appeal. Often his clients made comments that his paintings were a haven from daily stress.

I grew up watching him lightly brush a canvas. Magically, billowing clouds and deep mountain shadows emerged. One day, after I was grown, I stopped by, and he was working on a spectacular commission piece of the Superstition wilderness. We chatted about his work, and I joked that it wasn't fair that he got all the talent and I couldn't draw a straight line.

Being a man of few words, he said, "No man is born talented. Talent is the development of a God-given gift. God gives everyone a gift of talent. How well you use it will determine the degree of your talent."

Little did Dad know what a comfort those few words provided. For years, I felt that when God handed out talent, I was standing behind the door. Now I thought maybe that wasn't so, but how could I find out about my personal gift from God?

Most of us hope or wish God's gift would be something obvious. For me, He didn't wrap it in bright, shiny paper. I guess I'm a brown paper type of gal. For years, I stumbled over and passed over my gift. So, where did I find it? When I asked God to show me my gift, He directed to look in an area of my life where I received the greatest selfless pleasure. Alas, even though I wasn't destined to be an artist or musician, my gift was perfect for me. His gifts are numerous, and each is tailored to fill a basic need we all possess—namely, to contribute to the betterment of humankind for His glory.

To list them would be impossible, but here are a few places to look for your special gift.

Does your heart ache when you see starving children or a homeless person, or hear the feeble voice of a desperately ill person? Perhaps you have the gift of compassion or healing.

Do you willingly stop to help your neighbors or someone in need? It is a high calling to be a servant to humankind. Your gift may be to serve others.

Are you passionate about learning? The quest for wisdom can have a double purpose because inquisitiveness and teaching go hand and hand. The ability to impart knowledge is a wonderful gift and one that has a lasting impact.

Are you a good listener or judge of character? You may possess the gift of discernment and common sense. Oh, that there were more who might discover and develop this gift.

Do you love to read, journal, sew, or cook? Perhaps you could read to the blind, write devotions, make charity clothing or quilts, or prepare food for a family in crisis. This is a vital gift of sharing God's love.

Are you crafty, and do you look for the good in people? Perhaps you like to send cards, emails, or letters to people? You may possess the precious gift of encouragement.

Perhaps you possess an ability to earn money. With this gift comes tremendous responsibility. Developing this gift of philanthropy changes lives and is a blessed necessity.

God's gifts are innumerable and multifaceted. They make up who we are. We all have them. Regardless of your gift, if you listen to God, follow your heart, and develop your talent, it will become as great as He wants it to be. You may not be the next van Gogh, Einstein, Shakespeare, or Mozart, but you have talent nonetheless.

Praise You, Father, for imbuing Your children with good gifts. Let us remember to use them for the world to feel Your love, energize our desire to grow closer to You, and use them for Your glory.

Having gifts that differ according
to the grace given to us …
—Romans 12:6a ESV

RICE PUDDING

While waiting to check out at the market, I watched a young woman with three freshly scrubbed, small children fumble urgently through her coupons. Her grocery basket contained the bare essentials—a bag of beans, some soup, milk, bread, a jar of peanut butter, a pound of hamburger, a bar of soap, and a bag of rice. She carefully laid out the coupons for the peanut butter, soup, and rice. In her hand, she clutched two dollars and a food stamp card.

For some reason, it struck me that it was seven days before the end of the month, and I wondered if this would be all they had to eat before the first of next month. Guiltily, I looked in my basket filled to overflowing with fresh produce, frozen vegetables, a turkey, chicken breasts, pork chops, a roast, and some gourmet items and assorted other goodies. The little boy asked his mother if he could have a candy bar. The mother lovingly stooped down, kissed him, and said softly, "Not this time, but I will make you some rice pudding tomorrow for Thanksgiving. The youngster smiled and exclaimed to his siblings, "Mommy's making rice pudding for Thanksgiving!" The two smaller children clapped their hands and laughed.

After her meager groceries were bagged, she and the children left the store. I asked the clerk if she was a regular customer. He replied,

"Yes, and you couldn't find a nicer gal. Her husband was killed last year in a car wreck, and she is really having a tough time."

I turned and picked up a gift card for the grocery store and asked if he would run it first so I could catch her before she left. He did, and I chased after her. Her little boy was trailing behind, and I gave it to him and told him to give it to his mother. He looked at me and smiled and raced to catch up with her. I watched from inside the store as she looked at it and turned it over and looked around. She slipped it in her purse as tears ran down her face.

While the clerk rang up the rest of my groceries, the words of the song came to mind:

"Let Your Heart Be Broken"*

Let your heart be broken
A world in need;
Feed the mouths that hunger
Soothe the wounds that bleed,
Give a cup of water and a loaf of bread
Be the hands of Jesus;
Serving in His stead

As the tune played in my head, I thought about all those lonely, less fortunate homeless people who wander the streets and the unseen poor who are desperately trying to hang on. Then I realized that Thanksgiving has more than one meaning. It isn't just about giving thanks for God's bountiful blessing.

Thanksgiving is a compound word—thanks and giving. Saying thank you to the Lord is the easy part. The second part calls us to action, "to be the hands of Jesus," to be giving.

For many, the approximate four-week period from Thanksgiving to Christmas is our charitable season. It is a time when our hearts are pricked, but giving should not be a seasonal activity. This country is experiencing a time of great prosperity, and it is possible to reverse the downward spiral of the hurting and poor.

This Thanksgiving when we list our blessings, we should make a second list of ways we can be the hands of Jesus over the next year. For example, in July, can we afford to provide a treat for the homeless by purchasing and delivering five gallons of ice cream to a shelter? Can we encourage our friends and neighbors to do the same? Or, in February, can we afford to buy an additional twenty dollars of food or buy a gift card to give to someone in need? In August, how about purchasing some extra school supplies or a couple of pairs of shoes? Perhaps we could purchase a blanket or sweatshirts during the after-Christmas sales.

If you don't know anyone in need, just spend a little time near a checkout counter at the grocery store. You'll soon be able to spot those who could use help. Or, the alternative, contact community service organizations or a church in a less affluent neighborhood. They will gladly direct you.

If we, as the most prosperous nation in the world, can send a man to the moon and be leaders in scientific development and medical research, surely we can take care of our poor and homeless. Individually, we need only to look for the opportunity to make a difference. Collectively, if we each committed to be the hands of Jesus, those who are suffering from a variety of issues, such as being homeless, hungry, and cold or in need of mental or physical attention, would find that life is filled with the joys of helping others. Truly, there is nothing like it. Your Thanksgiving will truly be a time of thanks and giving.

And he said, "The one who showed mercy toward him."
Then Jesus said to him, "Go and do the same."
—Luke 10:37 NASB

COUSIN BILL

In the 1940s and '50s, our society was not nearly as mobile or sophisticated as it is today. It was not unusual for extended families to stay in one locale for their entire lives. My parents broke with that tradition when they moved from Indiana to Arizona. Every summer, however, we returned to the Midwest to visit with family and friends. Some of my fondest childhood memories revolve around such trips, especially because Cousin Bill lived there.

Bill was the only child of Aunt Marie and Uncle Ralph, and by all accounts, he was the most talented, most handsome, smartest boy ever born. Once, I overheard Mother talking to Grandma about how absolutely spoiled Bill was, but I didn't really understand what that meant, since I too was an only child and spoiled. To me, Bill was perfect. We had a special bond since both of us suffered from the only-child syndrome, and although we were cousins, we acted more like brother and sister.

In those days, life was far simpler. Washington was a small town where everyone knew everyone else and all of their business. Adults kept a watchful eye on all children, not just their own. Kids played on the sidewalks, walked to the corner grocery, and stopped along the way to visit with friends and neighbors. If you were lucky, they would offer a cold lemonade or piece of candy. People were more trusting, and violence didn't reign in the streets.

Even though Bill was ten years older, he took me everywhere. Our days and evenings were filled with adventure. We went to the river to fish, walked along the railroad tracks, played in the park, went to the movies, stopped by the drugstore for a cherry Coke, or simply sat on Grandma's back porch, talking and munching on fresh strawberries. Years passed, and Bill joined the army and was promptly sent to Korea. He was gone for two long years.

Oh, how I missed him. No one before or since could make me laugh like Bill. His quick wit, occasionally sarcastic and dry, was like candy to me. When he returned, we resumed our fun times. I went to his ballgames and watched in admiration and pride as Bill belted hits and home runs. His athletic prowess was legendary, and everyone just knew he would be scouted and called up to the big leagues. When that didn't happen, he left for college.

He had great entrepreneurial ambitions and set his sights on a business degree. Then he discovered a new talent and starred in several drama productions. He promptly changed his major and decided to become an actor.

Everyone knew it was just a matter of time before Hollywood discovered his comedic acting talent. That didn't happen either.

Instead, he married a flower child woman who no one really understood. Together they had a son with a genius IQ. His wife decided she wanted to be a pilot and abandoned both Bill and their son for the wild blue yonder. The marriage ended in divorce. Bill, however, was just too busy to seriously pursue fatherhood. Eventually, his parents assumed his responsibilities and moved to Florida to raise their grandson. After that, Bill rarely saw his son.

Then Bill decided to follow in his grandfather's footsteps and become a fireman, but he washed out after a year. His next venture was a fish stand, where he served up the best fish sandwiches ever known to man, but for Bill, it became boring, and he gave that up as well.

By far, Bill's greatest talent was his piano virtuosity. His musical compositions and ability to play rivaled the talent of Scott Joplin. Unbelievable talent, but other than playing at parties and in a few bars, he never pursued it as a career. Bill was so blessed and multitalented, yet he never seemed able to measure up to his potential. He always fell short.

In his later years, he wrote for the newspaper, and again, people recognized his pure comedic and quaint writing style. He remarried and told tall tales about fishing, the outdoors, and his experiences with his "long-suffering" wife. In particular, he shared her racoon stew recipe with the world.

A few years ago, we had a chance to have a long talk. I asked him if he still played the piano, and he said no. I asked if he was still doing community theater, and he said no. I asked if he was still fishing, and he said no. I asked if he was still coaching Little League teams, and he said no. Finally, I asked him what he was doing. He said, "Growing up."

I laughed. "At sixty-three?"

He paused and said, "You know, Sandy, when I was younger, I never understood the importance of obedience."

Confused, I asked, "What do you mean?"

"Unfortunately, I didn't learn the first rule of life. I skipped right past it. Obedience to God is the first rule of life. I played a game. I fooled a lot of people—my parents, my wife, my son, Grandma and Grandpa, you, your parents, Aunt Ethel, Uncle Ed, Aunt Marg, Uncle Enoch, and everyone else I met—but I didn't fool God. I didn't obey Him. He blessed me with so much raw talent, but I didn't appreciate it, develop it, or use it for His glory.

"Remember this, Sandy. Obedience is the first exercise in self-discipline, and discipline is the key to success. It all starts with being obedient to God. If you don't learn that, failure will be your constant companion."

I was at a loss for words. Finally, in an attempt to comfort him, I said, "Bill, you haven't failed. You still have your talents, not the least of which is being a good communicator. You just need to pass that bit of wisdom along to everyone you meet."

He just grinned that silly grin and winked. "What do you think I'm doing, kiddo?"

And his affection for you is even greater, as
he remembers, the obedience of you all, how
you received him with fear and trembling.
—2 Corinthians 7:15 ESV

KEEP THOSE CARDS AND LETTERS COMING

For years, we've mailed Christmas cards to friends and relatives and have always received a goodly stack in return. Dutifully, every New Year's Day, I updated my address book and added those who were first timers. In the past, the additions outstripped the deletions, but recently it seems the names dropped from our card list is growing faster. Those on the drop list usually bring tears, because these are friends who have passed away or disappeared because of divorce, moving out of state, and so on.

Being the pack rat that I am, I have collected shoeboxes full of Christmas cards from years past. Why? I don't know. Maybe because I like them; I thought they were pretty and couldn't part with them. They were from people I cared about and who cared about me.

Yesterday, while taking down Christmas decorations, packing, and repacking the shed, my husband brought in two big boxes filled with my card collection and gently suggested that I go through them to see if we really need them to make our life complete. (Obviously, he is the practical one of the family.)

This wasn't in my plan, but I decided he did have a point. I sat in the middle of the floor surrounded by shoeboxes. I organized them by sorting them into three stacks—family, friends, and business. (Yes, I kept the business cards!) Then I sorted them by name, alphabetically. Finally, I began to read the verses, notes, and letters.

There were a lot of those family-doings letters. Some were so old that the paper was yellow and the ink was faded. You notice, I mentioned *ink* (as in handwritten). These were almost holy relics of the time before computers and desktop publishing. These were legacies, family histories, and are priceless because someone took the time to share family news and express care for our family.

Of course, there were those cards with imprinted names and no handwritten notes. At one time, it was proper to send cards to everyone you knew, whether you liked them or not. Some of these cards bore names I didn't recognize. Apparently, we were on my B or C list.

Some of the business cards were funny. In fact, many of them are no longer in business. I laughed at one card that was signed by employees, all forty-five of them. I wondered what happened to those folks. What about those group-photo cards? Can you believe we ever looked like that? What a neat way to watch families grow up.

The older cards were less expensive, usually carried a true message about Christ's birth, contained handwritten notes, and had stamps that were only twelve cents. As the years passed, the people became busier (or perhaps I should say became more self-occupied), and the cards evolved. Now they were more sophisticated and elegant. The paper was heavier, and often they were enveloped in shiny foil. Most carried the noncommittal, politically correct message of "happy holidays." The computer-generated family-doings letter now became a bragging note.

I'm not a sociologist, but as I read these cards, it became painfully clear that people are less connected with friends and family than in the past. Fewer people are sending cards, and those bragging notes are filled with shallow messages of dribble and trivia about Harold's promotion, ski trips to Aspen, and upcoming cruise plans. Where are those ordinary letters filled with humor and self-deprecating stories about the fish that got away or an update on Uncle John's gout?

Many businesses have ceased sending cards. More than likely, it's too expensive. After all, fancy cards cost a couple of bucks or more (some as much of six dollars), and stamps are now fifty cents (for right now). Still, it is a great goodwill gesture and sure beats spending those advertising bucks on some cheap gimmick.

After spending the better part of the day reminiscing, the moment of truth arrived when my husband sauntered into the room and asked how it was going. He looked in the trash can, and there were a meager five cards. He just winked and said, "Hon, it's a start," and helped me repack my boxes to be put away for another year in our bulging shed.

I'm glad I saved those scraps of paper, because I am reminded how important it is to stay connected, even if only once a year. In the end, it makes little difference what the card looks like, what the verse says, or how the letter is written. The point is someone cared enough to share a bit of their life with you. Treasure it! Keep those cards and letters coming.

That these days should be remembered and
kept throughout every generation.
—Esther 9:28a ESV

Doin' and Workin'

Have you ever said, "There simply aren't enough hours in the day," or "I wish a day had thirty-six hours instead of twenty-four?" I find myself wishing for that thirty-six-hour day at least two or three times a week. These are days that start at five in the morning and end at ten or eleven at night. I have done nothing but shower, work, and maybe eat. Sometimes I subsist on coffee, tea, soda, and quick finger foods. Each day, my husband comes home for lunch and always catches me unaware. I'm surprised that six hours have passed.

Mine is not a problem of saying no or being unorganized. After many years, I finally mastered the art of saying no, and usually I can find the things I need within a few minutes. My problem is that there are just so many projects I want and like to do. I'm always doin' and workin'.

It's hard to believe, but at this writing, it is spring. In reviewing notes for this writing, I found I had drafted this piece back in 2002. This year from January to April, the days disappeared as fast as bubbles. It has been extremely busy between quilting, writing deadlines, and other responsibilities. I probably do my best work under deadline, but it does take its toll. As I complete each project, I only have a brief few minutes to reflect on and enjoy my accomplishment because another looming deadline waits to attack.

My life felt like that *I Love Lucy* candy factory assembly line—write a little, quilt a little, cook a little, laugh a little, reflect a little, nap very little, and keep doin' and workin'. For years, my dream job was to be a freelance writer and quilter. The Lord blessed me and gave the opportunity to do what I wanted, but the joy had slowly evaporated. I was just doin' and workin'.

At the beginning of the year, my husband and I made a commitment to read the Bible through in a year. We had done it a couple of years ago and so enjoyed it that we decided to do it again. It only takes about fifteen minutes a day. True to form and under the pressure of time constraints, it wasn't long before I was hopelessly behind in my readings. I started to play catch-up. Instead of fifteen minutes, I was up to thirty or more. Again, what was once enjoyable was no longer so. Life is definitely out of kilter when reading the Bible is not an uplifting experience.

The mood of dread, doom, and blues set in. I wondered if I had forever lost the pleasure of doing those things I so enjoyed. How could I keep from being too tired to appreciate the beauty of the day or the pleasure of my accomplishments? I questioned if it was worth the effort. Or should I give up and go back to a regular nine-to-five job? No pressure or deadlines there. Yeah, right!

The next day, when I sat down to read, I determined that, regardless of any deadline, I would not be rushed and that I would leisurely read until I was caught up with my readings. I decided that I would spend more time in meditation ... just waitin' and listenin' for God's voice. I don't know how long I sat there, but it must have been quite a while. I even wondered if I had dozed off because, for the first time in days, I felt refreshed, my mind was clear, and my heart was peaceful. That day lasted, I'm sure, at least thirty-six unhurried hours. Even though my project load was at its peak, I didn't feel pushed, rushed, or propelled to work. I got more done than usual. More importantly, I enjoyed what I was doing.

Even though I had spent more of my precious minutes meditating on God's Word, my strength was restored, and my soul was at ease.

I felt transformed. Words that had been stuck in the recesses of my mind began to flow. Quilts that I had been ripping apart because the points didn't match were now stitched accurately and easily. No longer was I fighting the clock and myself. The more I pondered this transformation, the more convinced I became that God's message to me was simply this: "Not so much doin' and workin', but a lot more waitin' and prayin.'"

How about you?

May my meditation be pleasing to Him,
for I rejoice in the Lord.
—Psalm 104:34 ESV

It's Christmas

Grandchildren have a way of asking questions that sometimes give us reason to pause before answering. As we started decorating for Christmas, my brilliant ten-year-old grandson wanted to know what made the Wise Men wise. He wanted to know where they went to school and what their job was and where they lived. Well, I was at a loss to really answer these questions, but it sent me on a quest. You can't disappoint a grandson; he expects an answer.

As I started to ruminate on his question, I realized there were a lot of lessons to be had in his innocent questions. When the Magi bowed before the baby Jesus, they brought more than three gifts of gold, frankincense, and myrrh. Beyond these temporal gifts, the Magi brought gifts of the heart.

First, they brought the gift of faith. It took enormous, faith to set out on such a perilous journey. For nearly two years, they traveled along caravan routes, fraught with danger and few amenities. Undaunted, they followed the star. They had faith that it would lead them to the newborn King.

Second, they gave the gift of humility. When they found Jesus in a humble dwelling, they were not deterred. They bowed before the Christ child in reverence and awe, for they recognized Him as the King of kings.

Third, they presented the gift of obedience. They were obedient to God's messenger when they were told not to return to Jerusalem or tell Herod the whereabouts of Jesus. They took a different route home.

When we give gifts at Christmas, we can take a lesson from the Wise Men. While we give temporal gifts, more importantly, we need to give gifts of the heart. Here is an easy way to remember just a few of the precious gifts Jesus gave to us and how we can share them with someone else:

Compassion. This gift will bring peace of heart to someone who is suffering. Be attuned to those who are hurting. Share this special gift with them. Christ showed His compassion for you when He went to the cross.

Hope. Everyone needs to know that despite life's anguishes and pain, there is hope for the future. Offer the gift of hope. Let them know that they are of value and tomorrow is another precious day. Jesus gave us all the gift of hope for eternal life when He freely gave his own life for ours.

Reconciliation. Do you have a strained relationship with someone? You can give them the blessed gift of reconciliation. Forgive and forget your differences, for life is too short to live with anger and bitterness. Jesus offered forgiveness to the thief, even as he was dying.

Integrity. This is a gift for a lifetime. By living your life with integrity, you set an example for all to follow. Integrity is learned. What better gift could you give to your child? You lead by example. Christ's life showed us how to live with integrity.

Steadfastness. Being a steadfast friend to those you love and know is worth its weight in gold. What a relief it is to know that when the going gets rough, you have a steadfast friend. Christ is such a friend. He is always there through the good times and the bad.

Time. Giving your time to others is one of the most precious gifts you can bestow. Take time to visit your neighbor, listen to a child, visit with someone who is lonely, or donate your time to a program that reaches out into the community to help those less fortunate. Where would we be if Jesus had said, "Sorry, I have to go. I don't have time"?

Mercy. A merciful heart seeks to go the extra mile. Look for opportunities to put aside your own desires and prejudices and show mercy to someone who might not "deserve" it. We didn't deserve God's grace and mercy, but Jesus more than showered us with both.

Attitude. The gift of a good attitude will spread throughout your family and workplace. Give everyone this gift and watch it grow and multiply. It is hard to not return a smile. Likewise, it is hard to have a bad attitude when surrounded with people who have good attitudes. No matter how tired he was, Jesus always exhibited patience and a good attitude.

Selflessness. This gift can change the world. For by your actions, you will be known. Stop, look, and listen is the game plan for a selfless person. Seeking no recognition, go out of your way to ascertain the needs of someone else. Jesus performed the ultimate act of selflessness when He took upon the sins of the world and died for you and me.

"Bear fruits in keeping with repentance ..."
—Luke 3:8 ESV

GODLY SURPRISES

Often, we are given little gifts from friends and relatives that have a much bigger impact on us than the giver might ever know. I received such a gift from a dear friend. It was a lovely devotional book with a quilting theme. It is entitled *Patterns of Grace*, written and compiled by Roy Lessin and Heather Solum. I read the entire book on the plane and thoroughly enjoyed it. It is filled with thought-provoking sayings and stories. When I returned home, I added to my devotional book collection.

My daughter asked if I would accompany her and her four "absolutely precious, highly intelligent, articulate" children on a sojourn to Sea World and the San Diego Zoo. Of course, I said yes. What grandmother wouldn't?

As we entered Sea World Park, my precocious granddaughter stood patiently as I slathered her with sunscreen. We were standing near the big tank where Shamu resided. Her eyes grew wide as she got her first look at "Shampoo" (a.k.a. Shamu). During the show, she sat transfixed watching the whale's antics and listening to the trainers. What a special moment to see pure wonderment in a child's eyes.

We traipsed around from one venue to another. At the Artic Adventure, we stood before the window gazing upon the beautiful white beluga whales. This little girl of four stood there with a look of puzzlement on her face. Finally, she turned to me and in a very grown-up voice asked, "Nana, where are their dorsal fins? I was absolutely amazed that she recognized that significant difference between the two whale species. And, at that point, I hadn't noticed their lack of dorsal fins, let alone questioned why they did not have dorsal fins. I needed to find an answer for this sweetie. So, I pulled out my phone and quickly found out. They don't have dorsal fins because they would be a hinderance and cause loss of heat when the whales are surfacing in loose packed ice. So says Google.

The following day, we headed for the San Diego Zoo. As we got out of the car, both she and her three-year-old sister reminded their mother and me that we had forgotten to put on the "scumstream." Yet another special moment that brought giggles to my heart.

On Monday, it was off to the beach. Personally, I love the ocean but really don't care for the discomfort of a sandy swimsuit. Again, a blessing awaited me. My sixteen-month-old grandson's first experience with sand and sea was a sight to behold. It only happens once in a lifetime, and I was fortunate to be there to see him play with such abandon as the ocean washed up and over his legs and back out to sea, and I listened to his giggles and watched him stamp his feet. Needless to say, all of the children were absolute messes, but their joy was too great to be concerned about how we would ever get the sand out of the hair or the car. For me, to observe the incredible beauty of childhood freedom was a special gift from God.

As I reflected upon the trip, I recalled the book my friend had given me. I started to reread it in search of those wonderful words that had blessed me before. Now they had much more meaning than before. The quote was "God has something new for you every day; He delights in you and loves to surprise you with good things."

He certainly surprised me on this trip by capturing the sweetness and innocence of childhood. I felt renewed, refreshed, and younger to have had the opportunity to look at life through a child's eyes. As we grow older, I fear that we stop seeking godly surprises. If we would only look for them each day, our lives, like those of children, would be filled with wonderment, awe, and delight. Who knows? This just might be the fountain of youth.

Blessed are the people to whom such blessings fall!
Blessed are the people whose God is the Lord!
—Psalm 144:15 ESV

A FREE AND EASY CURE

A few weeks ago, my husband came home from work feeling puny and complained of being achy and lightheaded. Using my best doctorial techniques, I diagnosed the flu and prescribed lots of fluids and rest. As he rested, watching the NBA playoffs, I continually refilled his water glass, and within a couple of hours, he fully recovered. What appeared to be the flu was, in fact, dehydration. This incident caused me to ponder my own fluid intake. While I was drinking a lot of other fluids and a sip of water here and there, I had not drunk a glass of water in weeks.

Over the next few days, I forced myself to drink at least eight to ten glasses of water a day. I fully believed that I would float away and then my bladder would burst. However, to my astonishment, my joints stopped aching. I had no nighttime muscle cramps. I slept better, lost a little weight, and my skin was smoother.

Then, recently, we spent a few days high in the Colorado Rockies. As we carried our things from the car to the room, my gait slowed, and finally I could go no farther. Lightheaded, breathing hard, I collapsed on the bed. Concerned, my husband called the front desk. They told him I was suffering altitude sickness and that I should drink a lot of water. After downing four glasses of water, my symptoms disappeared. Although not dehydrated, I needed more oxygen, and drinking the water gave a quick and effortless way to oxygenate my body. Again, water was key.

Fascinated by these water-related incidents, I looked up articles on dehydration and was surprised to learn that nearly two-thirds of the population is chronically dehydrated. As desert dwellers, we should be even more aware of the importance of water. No amount of coffee, tea, soda, beer, or other drinks can supply the body's need for water. Sometimes, even though we know this to be true, we forget and neglect our bodies. By the time we become thirsty, we are already dehydrated, since thirst is only an indicator that your reserves are low. If properly hydrated, there will be no thirst. Learning to drink water in quantity is a conscious effort that eventually becomes a good habit, one that will keep us refreshed and our bodies renewed. And soon you will crave water rather than coffee, tea, or soft drinks.

Likewise, the same can be said about spiritual dehydration. Again, we recognize the malaise but easily explain away the symptoms. For example, tension, stress, depression, frustration, and anger are attributed to a job, coworkers, family members, finances, and other events in our lives. There are thousands of drugs available to ease our discomfort, but they do not cure the problem. Our spiritual thirst is indicative of low reserves of faith and hope.

The degree of physical and spiritual dehydration runs the gamut from mild to severe. By far, however, the worse form of dehydration is chronic as we continually operate on a subpar level. Just as a thirsty body suffers, so does a thirsty soul.

The cure is available and free for the taking. As our bodies are restored by drinking quantities of water, our souls are refreshed by drinking long and deep from God's Word and allow the Living Water to infuse our soul. Going to the well of God's Word is a conscious effort, and when practiced, it, too, becomes a good habit. Daily Bible study, prayer, and meditation time are necessary elements for our spiritual survival. And we will find that our world desires will lesson as well.

When we quench our thirst with physical water and the Living Water, we enable our bodies and souls to function at peak performance. Truly, both waters are critical for a healthy, balanced, fulfilled, and purposeful life.

Let anyone who is thirsty come to me and drink.
Whoever believes in me, as Scripture has said,
rivers of living water will flow from them.
—John 7:37–38 NIV

A Mending Spirit

Do any of you remember the old embroidered tea towels? You know the ones I mean—weekly towels embroidered with Wash on Monday, Iron on Tuesday, Sew on Wednesday, Market on Thursday, Clean on Friday, Bake on Saturday, and Rest on Sunday?

My mother lived by this code of conduct. On Mondays, she stripped the beds, collected up dirty clothes, towels, and other linens, and spent the day washing. Before dryers were available, she proudly filled her clothesline for all the world to see that she was doing her job.

Tuesday started with sprinkling down her clothes and preparing them for ironing. I am old enough to remember when there were no steam/spray irons. And, I might add, she ironed everything we wore, from Dad's boxers to tablecloths. She even ironed our sheets. Can you even imagine?

Wednesdays were Mother's favorite day (next to Sundays). My mother always had a basket near her chair where she had such items as holey socks, broken zippers, worn-out pockets, items missing buttons. It was her mending basket. She believed that until something was totally threadbare, it had value. And even in its final death throes, it still had value as a rag. She rarely ever mended anything with her sewing machine. She preferred to just sit and work away, needle in hand.

As a young wife and mother, I tried to keep her schedule. After all, she was my example. Well, like her, I didn't have a dryer. I used cloth diapers, and washing diapers was an ongoing issue, not just on Mondays. I was doing well to wash our other clothing and linen. I rarely got everything washed by Tuesday. Now I was a day behind before I ever began. My mending basket grew into a mountain, because I was ironing on Wednesday. You get the picture, right? I just couldn't maintain that schedule.

One day, she came over and asked if I needed help. I guess my wild hair and the dark circles under my eyes were a dead giveaway. I now had two babies in diapers and was helping my husband. We owned a bakery, which meant very, very early hours of doughnut frying and helping with customers, with the wee ones in a playpen nearby.

It was then she looked at my mending basket and exclaimed, "Sandy, you're not going to have anything to wear if you don't get to that mending." At that point, I just didn't care, and since she offered, I flippantly said, "Be my guest," as I pointed to the stack. She smiled and said, "I'd love to."

That wasn't exactly the reply I expected. She promptly set about the task of doing my mending. She insisted that I make a pot of coffee and sit for a while. She wouldn't let me touch the mending but just wanted me to sit and chat for a while. What a wonderful hour we shared. I felt refreshed and hadn't done a thing.

A few years later, she continued to march her weeks away in spite of the of the newfangled dryer and the arrival of polyester and wash-and-wear clothing that did not require ironing—never forgetting Dad's boxers and the pillowcases that did need to be ironed. And she always found mending to do. Some of mine, some of friends, church needs, and neighbors who knew how she loved to make new things from old cloth. One Wednesday, I asked her if she ever got tired of mending. And her answer was, "No, I don't."

"Why?" I asked.

With a little poetic license, she said something to the effect of this: "Mending is more than just darning a hole in something, or sewing up a rip or tear, or putting on a button. It's rescuing something that was once beautiful and worthy and that is now tattered and torn, faded, and worn out, and remembering it has seen better days. When I mend, it's like I have a hand in restoring it to good purpose and deed. Sometimes that is a challenge, but when I am done, I feel like I have accomplished something."

My mom had a mending spirit. You see, she took the principle of mending to other parts of her life. She loved to help those who were torn or broken, those whose lives were fading, and those who were tattered by life's struggles. Sometimes it was simply remembering those who were broken with a kindness, or a card, or offering a listening ear, or helping someone who was tattered come to see that they could be made brand-new by Jesus. Yes, she could look at someone and see how beautiful they had been—and could be again. She just loved to put a little stitch into their restoration.

It makes me wonder, What if we all developed a little mending spirit? I think the world would look refreshed, renewed, revived, and reborn.

I will show kindness to Hanun son of Nahash,
because his father's kindness to me …
—1 Chronicles 19:2 NIV

THE INFLUENCE OF A COMMON MAN

During a writing workshop, the instructor gave his students an exercise meant to develop their skills for writing succinctly. The assignment was to write, in twenty words or less, an epitaph for a family member's grave marker, summarizing the deceased's life.

For my dad, I wrote, "A man of God, a good husband, a loving father, a common man of influence."

There it was in fifteen words. My dad. His paintings were precise and realistic. Such attention to detail, shading, and depth produced near-photographic images. Yet he meticulously brushed away life's ugly imperfections, leaving only the exquisite beauty of life.

Unexpectedly, at sixty-four, Dad died of a massive coronary. In the days following his death, Mother and I were amazed by the volume of calls we received from people around the country. They called to express their sympathy and to inquire if we were selling any of his paintings. We received calls from two greeting card companies expressing interest in acquiring the rights to use his paintings on their merchandise.

At first, we were a bit off put that people seemed so callous and mercenary during the worst days of our lives, but as the calls poured in, we noticed an overlying message in their calls. We started to journal the comments, and eventually, these remarks became the bedrock of our comfort.

"Rolland's paintings are so full of hope."

"When I look at one of his paintings, there is such serenity."

"He knew how to bring peace and tranquility to art."

"His work touched my soul."

"He captured God's handiwork on canvas."

"Rolland understood the beauty of the simple things in life."

And, "I've never seen 'peace' painted before."

It has been nearly forty years since he died, and recently, I received yet another call asking if I had any of my father's paintings for sale. Once again, the caller reaffirmed Dad's impact through his paintings. He said, "Whenever I look at Rolland's painting, I see what God intended for us to enjoy on this earth. When I'm down, I spend some time with your dad's painting, and my spirit is always lifted." Reflecting on this call, I thought of Dad's legacy and his quiet influence. He had a gift for translating to canvas the beauty of nature and the purity of God's creation.

Most of us are just common folk, like my dad, but each of us possess a gift from God. Maybe it is a gift of remarkable artistry and creativity (like my daughter Erika's), the gift of teaching (like my daughter Heidi's), the gift of compassion and humor (like my son, Rolland's), or the gift of special love (like my daughter Monika's love for animals). Let's remember a gift is not a gift until it is given away. Do you have gifts that can be shared? Obviously, my dad understood this. His love of God and his sense of peace still influence those who are fortunate to own one of his paintings. What a blessing! Thank you for sharing your gift with others and with me.

And he must have a good reputation with
those outside the church, so that he will not
fall into reproach and the snare of the devil.
—1 Timothy 3:7 NASB

PLAYING WITH PAPER DOLLS

If you were a little girl in the 1950s, '60s, and to some degree in the '70s, you probably were enthralled with the iconic joy of playing paper dolls. These lovelies usually came in a booklet wherein the dolls, dressed in their underwear, were on the thicker paper of the covers, and the booklet was filled with fantastic clothing items, each having little white tabs to fold over to hold the clothes on.

Hours were required to carefully punch out the dolls and carefully cut out each outfit and all of the accessories. Long before there were baggies, my mother provided me with large manila clasp envelopes to keep my dolls and their clothing nice and flat. I put the name of each doll on the front and with caution laid in their clothing. It wasn't long before I had a large number of these big envelopes.

My father, the engineer and artist, decided to sit with me as I cut out yet another set of clothes for a new paper doll. Before long, he had carefully drawn what appeared to be stitching around the envelope and sketched travel labels. With great care, he colored them, and my envelopes magically evolved into suitcases.

If the truth be known, my mother loved my paper dolls almost as much as I did. Being an only child, I had a propensity to be a chatterbox. Literally, hours would pass as I dressed my dolls, went shopping and to parties with the other dolls, and, of course, traveled the world to match my travel labels. Yes, these dolls were my best friends, and what adventures we had.

My dad became intrigued by my imagination and how I set up very primitive scenes in which my girls could play. He decided that he could build a table and make a miniature village complete with stores, town square, trees, rocks, cars, traffic light, and so on. We worked on it together. I remember several Saturdays we worked in the basement all day. I would hold light poles while he glued them into place, and I got to choose where to put trees. It wasn't long before Mother was drafted to make awnings for the buildings.

Now, from this simple, innocuous beginning grew more tabletop scenes in various countries. I had one for Rome, complete with the coliseum, a Vatican, and a road out of town known as the Appian Way. We spent weeks choosing locations and learning about our newest destinations. Another tabletop was Paris, another for London, another for St. Petersburg in Russia, New York, and Washington, DC. All around the basement, we had card tables, each another destination. (I never thought about it before, but I wonder where all those card tables came from.) As we worked and talked, I learned so much about these cities and countries. Magically, Daddy created tourist sites complete with restaurants, the Louvre, and Norte Dame in Paris; Harrods Department Store, Big Ben, and the Tower of London in London; and a bullfighting ring in Madrid. Mother jumped in and learned about the local cuisine, and we ate the food of the region, together with menus and decoration. The simple booklets of paper dolls turned into a family hobby.

By the time my paper doll obsession began to wane, we had seventeen little worldwide tabletop scenes. I recalled this recently when going through some of my huge quilting stash. There is a common quilt pattern called Sun Bonnet Sue. I had always planned to make a quilt utilizing this pattern in dressing the Sun Bonnet Sue in native costumes. I guess the idea is a throwback to playing with paper dolls.

Now, sixty-five-plus years later, here I was again dressing dolls. Fabric ones instead of paper. I designed clothes and developed and wrote a series of classes called Sun Bonnet Sue Travels the World. Within just a few days, I was transported back to the research we did on the various regions for our tabletop scenes. I luxuriated in warm thoughts and memories of time spent with my parents.

As I reflect on those wonderful times with my parents, I am reminded of how Jesus asked that the little children be allowed to come unto Him. His kindness and love were evident by the fact He *wanted* to spend time with them, just like my parents *wanted* to spend time with me.

My parents set an example by finding ways to be in my life, to spend time with me rather than leaving me to my own devices. In our current techy world, perhaps we need to find a way to be a part of our children's lives and not let them be alone in their virtual world.

We need to let them know we care about what they are interested in and that it is important to us. The alternative is truly bleak—no memories, no lessons learned, no laughter at failures or delight in successes, just an empty vacuum of meaningless electronic games and, in truth, a very lonely childhood.

Let's dedicate ourselves to loving our children, grandchildren, great-grandchildren with an intensity that shows the same love of Jesus. Regardless of the time you have, you can listen and talk with them. Keep them near, not hidden away in their rooms.

You shall teach them diligently to your children,
and shall talk of them when you sit in your
house, and when you walk by the way, and
when you lie down, and when you rise.
—Deuteronomy 6:7 ESV

An Advent Surprise

For several years, our church prepared a book of Advent devotions for families to read and share in preparation for the holy season of Christmas. Each year, I looked forward to this book of treasured thoughts and was devastated when the church stopped printing the book. How could I possibly get ready for Christmas without these wonderful daily devotions? They were as much a part of Christmas as the tree, nativity, or presents. Little did I know what a blessing awaited me.

That year, when the first day of Advent arrived, I was lost. Whatever was I to do? On Christmas Eve, it is our family tradition to read, by candlelight, the Christmas story before we start our family festivities. I decided to replace the void left from not having the Advent devotionals with memorizing the scriptures detailing the birth of Christ. Then on Christmas Eve, I could recite the story rather than read it. That was my intent, but it wasn't God's plan. Even though the Christmas story was so familiar, when I started to study the verses, it was as if I were reading them for the first time. Within a few minutes, I was highlighting passages in my Bible and jotting down notes and thoughts about the verses I read. Later in the day as I mulled over these scribblings, I watched the Living Word come alive with new revelations.

Upon a cursory reading, the greatest story ever told is a simple one. But when the verses are dissected, there are much deeper lessons and messages. On this particular day, the first revelation that hit me was the awesome faith of the Magi. Just imagine what travel was like in biblical times. Most people walked from place to place. The more fortunate might ride on donkeys, horses, or camels.

If you've ever been to the Phoenix Zoo and had opportunity to ride a camel, you know that it is a rough ride, at best. Even for the Wise Men, caravan travel was anything but luxurious.

It is believed the Magi came from Persia. To reach Bethlehem, they crossed hundreds of miles of the world's most forbidding terrain. Yet, with belief that defies human understanding, the Magi started their journey, fervent in their belief that the fulfillment of a prophecy was at hand. Guided only by a star, they sought the King of the Jews. A lesson in faith. Later, we see they obeyed an angelic warning not to divulge the child's whereabouts. A lesson in obedience.

On the second day of Advent, again I reread the story, and again the same thing happened. Soon, I was scribbling more notes and thoughts. Another message of incredible faith was highlighted when I read how Joseph arose from his sleep and immediately followed the angel's command that he take Mary and the small child, Jesus, and go into Egypt. He did not waver and did as instructed. A lesson in following the lead of the Holy Spirit.

By the third day, the pattern was set: read, try to memorize the verses, reflect, and write. On this day, I dug into the more familiar story of the divine faith. Imagine that you were thirteen or fourteen years of age and had been visited by the archangel Gabriel. That visitation would have challenged the faith of many. Beyond that, Mary's faith endured when she was told that was chosen to bear and deliver God's salvation for the world. Although there is no mention of her parents, can you imagine how their faith was tested when she told them she was with child?

Over the next few days, I looked at my writing and realized that, unwittingly, I was journaling my own Advent devotional guide. Never before had I understood and appreciated the divine gift of faith or felt the spirit of Christmas more fully.

Now, years later, this has become a personal Christmas tradition. Each year when I think there can't be twenty-four more new insights in the Christmas story, there are. What started as a loss turned out to be one of my greatest blessings. Try as I might, I still haven't gotten the story memorized.

Originally, when I started to write this parable, I planned to share one of my Advent devotionals, but, as usual, God had another plan. As the writing began to flow, it became clear that I should share the joy of writing an Advent journal and, hopefully, encourage others to try it. You will receive no greater Christmas gift. Beyond your own pleasure and enjoyment, your Advent journals become a tremendous legacy for your children and grandchildren. You and your family will be immeasurably blessed as you discover new truths in this blessed story.

My little children, I am writing these things
to you so that you may not sin. But if anyone
does sin, we have an advocate with the
Father, Jesus Christ the righteous.
—1 John 2:1 ESV

FROM SUNRISE TO SUNSET

My day started before dawn. Appointments, deadlines, and work that needed urgent attention lay ahead of me. I grabbed a cup of coffee and decided that I needed some quiet time on the back porch. The air was cool but not cold as I watched the coming sunrise. The softness and gentleness of the morning light was soothing. The soft, glistening light became bright, and God's alarm clock burst forth as the sun broke the horizon. The day brought more than a normal amount of opportunities and challenges. As evening approached, I was still editing a speech I was to deliver later on generational ministries.

This hectic day drew to a close when I slipped on a purple dress and donned a red hat. I looked more than a little strange. My red hat was a large-brimmed, feather-flying creation. I was to speak at a group of Red Hatters, a women's organization based on the poem "Warning" by Jenny Joseph. These groups of women are identified by their purple dresses and red hats. (In fact, this book is based on the same poem.)

While driving to my speaking engagement, I witnessed another of God's daily blessings. Living in Arizona, we often see this exquisite gift—an incredibly vibrant sunset. With the car windows down, I started to sing. At the top of my lungs, I bellowed out the words to "Sunrise, Sunset" from *Fiddler on the Roof.*

I probably should have had a bit more decorum and not encouraged road rage, but I felt like singing. Promptly, I started to bawl as much as I bellowed. I cried not in sadness but in joy. My tears were for the beauty of life and for the richness of the sunset. Of course, my epiphany played havoc with my makeup, necessitating a complete redo in the parking lot. I already looked strange enough, and I didn't need to scare them to death with black streaks running down my cheeks.

I had a great deal of difficulty concentrating on anything after that. I kept thinking about that glorious sunset. Arizona sunsets are a photographer's treasure. The evening sky literally glows in powerful shades of gold and amber, pink and rose. The silhouettes of majestic mountains and ageless cactus add a dimension of tranquility to the otherwise fiery sky.

What makes the sunsets so glorious? Dirt! That's it. Dirt! In order to get those rich pink shades, there must be dust in the air. Isn't it amazing that even dirt becomes beautiful when God touches it? But that's another whole life lesson.

I just couldn't contain myself during the business portion of the meeting. I grabbed my pen and furiously started scribbling on some napkins. I was writing God's message for me that day. Simply, it was that I should never belabor or begrudge the opportunities and challenges that come my way.

A few years ago, I attended a seminar where I was told that there are no problems, only opportunities. While this is a positive philosophy, from now on, I will refer to my "opportunities" as "sunset dust." That image helps me visualize that there is beauty at the end of my struggle.

At the rate I've been going, when I get old enough to face my sunset, it should be a doozie.

They who dwell in the ends of the earth
stand in awe of Your signs; You make the
dawn and the sunset shout for joy.
—Psalm 65:8 NASB

TALE OF THREE TREES

Hawaii is touted as a paradise on earth. This is almost true, with one notable exception: finding a nice fresh Christmas tree. Because the trees are cut early and shipped in by ocean freighter, they arrive in less than fresh condition and are quite costly.

One Christmas, we unpacked our ten-year-old, dilapidated artificial tree, hoping to get another year's use out of it. We decorated it, and when the lights were turned on, it was truly a pathetic sight. With its distorted and missing limbs, it was obvious that this was the year of its demise. We decided to purchase a live tree.

My husband left on a quest to find a new tree. Triumphantly, he returned with a scrawny little pine tree. When he brought it in, my heart sank. It was even uglier and more misshapen than the artificial tree. Its trunk was gnarled and crooked, and if you brushed against it, a cascade of dried needles fluttered to the floor, not to mention the big holes on three sides. After convincing my husband that the artificial tree was unacceptable and asking him to dismantle it, I thought it prudent to keep my displeasure to myself.

Our daughters, however, did not have the same reservations, and they protested vehemently. They unabashedly declared that this tree was, without a doubt, the ugliest tree they had ever seen. After a heated discussion, we decided to make this tree work, one way or another. The rest of the afternoon was spent decorating the tree and taking particular care to string the lights without completely baring the limbs of their dried needles and placing ornaments in such a manner as to fill the gaping holes. When we finished, it was obvious that this was a tree without merit. We even ran fishing line from the tree to our jalousie window cranks in an effort to straighten it up a bit. No matter what we did, it was still ugly.

After a couple of days, things got worse. Not only did the needles continue to fall at an alarming rate, the sagging bottom branches now touched the floor. Throwing my earlier prudence to the wind, I broached the subject of taking down yet another tree. My husband merely lay back in his recliner, crossed his arms, closed his eyes, and didn't say a word. This was not a good sign. Obviously, he was burrowing into his foxhole.

As we sat in silence, an orange whirlwind tore up the hall and climbed to the top of this fragile tree. Our cat, Spicy, dug her claws into the pencil-thin upper branches, and the tree began to whip back and forth. Scared, Spicy started her descent. The tree shuttered and crashed to the floor. Tangled in the lights and fishing line, she thrashed about, reeking even more havoc. Recognizing that the tree was now on the endangered list, my husband turned and asked, "How did you train her to do that?"

Again, we undecorated another tree. Later that day, the girls and I went shopping for a new tree and found a perfect, regal, noble fir tree. After overcoming the sticker shock, we headed home. The ugly little tree was carelessly thrown aside and lay on the lanai. With such a superior tree, we needed more elaborate ornaments and lots more lights. By now, the cost of the new tree ornaments, lights, and the tree itself reached the point of ridiculous. Even so, our anticipation was great as we started to decorate the noble tree. The result was a spectacular, department store, picture-perfect Christmas tree.

Later that evening when a friend stopped by, we proudly showed off our gorgeous tree. After she made her obligatory oohs and ahs, we sat on the lanai and visited. There in a heap was the little, ugly tree.

Julia turned and said, "Sandy, that is such a beautiful little tree. Why didn't you use it?" I told her the saga of our trio of trees.

As the evening progressed, she repeated her admiration for the little ugly tree. Finally, I stood the tree up, pointed out its many deficits, and asked, "Now, how can you call this pathetic excuse for a tree beautiful? It is just plain ugly."

She just smiled and, with tears in her eyes, said, "Sandy, it's a beautiful tree. It's God's tree. A tree to be decorated in honor of His Son's birth. All Christmas trees are beautiful, especially when you don't have one."

I knew Julia was having a rough time but never once considered that she might not have a tree. I asked her if she wanted the little tree. She quickly accepted. She took it home and decorated it. In her loving hands, it was transformed into a thing of beauty. As for my regal and perfect tree, its luster and beauty faded and paled in comparison.

The wisdom of a friend and the little tree reminded me that all things, if handled with love, become beautiful. What blessed assurance it is to know that God so loved us that He sent His Son to remove our ugliness and make us beautiful in His sight.

Postscript: To this day, we have a tiny little Charlie Brown tree with one ornament, which we use as reminder to look beyond outside and look for the inner beauty that God sees.

But Godliness actually is a means of great
gain with accompanied by contentment.
—1 Timothy 6:6 NIV

In the Shadow of an Angel's Wings

No one can deny that there is something special about the Christmas holidays. During this season, I sense that God opens the gates of heaven so we can behold the splendor of His home and catch a glimpse of the heavenly hosts that announced Christ's birth.

In 1970, two days before Christmas, I definitely felt the flutter of wings and caught a glimpse of God's messenger. With three children under six and expecting our fourth baby, I was frazzled. The gifts had been purchased but still needed to be wrapped, and I was racing to get the baking done. Despite my meticulous planning (a wee laugh here), every waking hour was filled with the minutiae of Christmas tasks.

On this particular day, I made one final push to finish the baking and candy making. My one-year-old daughter, Heidi, awoke from her nap with a flushed face and runny nose. When I checked her temperature, sure enough, she had a fever. I gave her a dose of baby aspirin and thought, *No! No! She can't be sick at Christmas.*

Around eight o'clock that night, I bathed the other children and put them in bed. Because Heidi's temperature continued to climb, I set up a port-a-crib and cool steam vaporizer near the kitchen door so I could keep an eye on her.

As I scooped out another ball of dough, I felt a strange rush of air, similar to a door being blown ajar, and saw a shadowy flash of a small child run past Heidi's crib.

I called (more accurately, I yelled) to my other children, "Rolland, Monika, quit running around and get in bed." Fully expecting to hear the flurry of feet and jumping on beds, I was surprised to hear nothing but silence and their distant reply.

"I'm in bed, Mama," Monika answered.

Rolland chimed in, "Me too."

There was no way they could be in bed.

Only seconds before, I saw one of them run by. I crossed the kitchen to Heidi's crib. When I looked in her crib, she lay perfectly still and blank, fixed eyes staring up at me. Her beautiful face had a strange grayish hue, and her lips were blue. I laid my hand on her chest and, in horror, realized she was not breathing. I grabbed her up and screamed for my husband. He took her from me and raced to the bathroom and started a very crude form of CPR while I called for an ambulance. (There was no 911 system or EMTs in those days, just an ambulance and a driver.)

My husband used a combination of breathing in her mouth and throwing water in her face to revive her. Suddenly, she gave a strangled gasp and started breathing again. Her color slowly returned, but her skin remained very hot.

The ambulance and police arrived, and Heidi was whisked away. She had a rough journey to the hospital. She started to convulse and stopped breathing two more times. Both times, she was revived by my primitive CPR attempts. At last we arrived at the hospital, where her care passed to a wonderful staff of doctors and nurses. Throughout the night of December 23, her little body struggled with the high fever, and she continued to have fibril convulsions.

Suddenly, those zillions of unfinished Christmas tasks were totally unimportant. We knelt by her hospital bed and simply prayed for our daughter's life. Near dawn, her fever began to subside, dropping from 105.2º to 103º. I don't ever recall being so happy to see a child's temperature reach 103°, but it was significant because, at 103°, she ceased to convulse. Heidi was diagnosed with a common childhood disease, roseola. Her little body simply could not handle the high fever that normally accompanies this illness.

On the morning of December 24, I sat in one of those less than comfortable hospital chairs, cradling Heidi and quietly singing praises to God for sparing our child. Once again, I felt that rush of cool air and looked into the hospital hallway and saw the wisp of a child's shadow pass the door. Then I realized that an intervening angel sent by God had passed by Heidi's crib to draw my attention to her battle for life. Now that she was better, the angel moved on to help someone else.

As my thoughts crystallized, I felt such a sense of awe. The realization that God's messenger moved within my home and touched my family was overwhelming. In this case, there was a physical presence, but throughout life, we frequently move in the shadow of angel wings.

God is always faithful to meet our needs. He uses many different means to reach us. It might be the still, quiet voice of answered prayer, or He may dispatch the angels to dramatically show us the way. At other times, when we stray, they may come to discipline us. Their power lies in the power of the Creator. Stay alert, for when you feel the flutter of the wings, you are standing in the shadow of God's power.

The angel of the Lord, encamps around
those who fear him, and delivers them.
—Psalm 34:7 NIV

So, Who Am I?

When I was two and a half, I was adopted.

That sentence bears more words in it than you would find in a novel. Not only does it define me, my life, my parents, and all of my relatives (biological and adopted), but more importantly, it describes me spiritually.

As a child, being adopted meant nothing to me. I had a mother and daddy and a good life. As I grew older, I took it for granted that I had other relatives in my life who were not really a part of my family.

At times, this was a bit confusing when I would go to visit Grandma Graham at her beauty shop and she introduced me by saying, "This is Sandy, Dick's daughter. Don't you think she looks like him?" And most everyone would agree that I had his eyes and hair and was the spitting image of him. At this point, I had no idea who Dick was. However, it eventually became clear to me. Dick was my biological father who had been killed in an automobile accident when I was a baby.

Life continued, and I basked in the honored position of being an only child. In that time period, 1940s and '50s, open adoption was as rare as a sweet lemon. Every trip back to Indiana, I had a double set of relatives to visit. Again, I was the princess in both families. My self-esteem never lacked for boosting. I visited with relatives on my biological father's side of the family. Not much of anything was said about my biological mother other than family gossip, and even that was pretty sketchy and lacking detail.

When I was an adult, things became more muddled. Gone was the childhood clarity of being the princess of two families, no questions asked. The devil in the details began to cause me to question, Was being adopted a stigma and really not such a good thing? Why was I adopted? Was I not a good girl? Why didn't they love me enough to keep me? Was I really as lucky as my parents said I was because they adopted me? Was I just a showpiece for my infertile parents? And what happened to my biological mother? Was she alive? Did I have any half brothers or sisters? The longer I lingered in this morass, I began to lose my self-esteem, my sense of worth, my ability to cope successfully. I grew to doubt everything I believed, including my belief in God. How could a loving God allow a child to be thrown aside to be picked up by someone else? Who could I talk to about these thoughts? Certainly not my adopted parents. I couldn't break their hearts by searching for answers. They were good, kind, and loving parents, except they had unrealistic expectations for me in all areas of my life. I couldn't hurt them with questions and by seeking more information regarding my biological family.

My parents both passed away within six months of each other when I was in my midthirties. I was free now to pursue my quest for information about my biological family. Yet I held back. I was suddenly frightened by what I might find. And my spirit continued to spiral downward. My antenna was up, scanning all that was said to find a way out of this pit of confusions and doubt.

Although I had attended church all my life, had accepted Jesus, had been baptized, and had a pretty fair understanding, I discovered I had never really allowed Him to be Lord of my life. I was in my mid to late thirties in my search for truth. I didn't want to start something that might hurt my young family. I returned to church with a burning desire to learn how to do that. Immersed in a Bible study, I met a wonderfully kind woman named Mrs. Coffer. She was a terrific Bible study leader. She seemed to understand her students and lead them through the maze of learning the Bible.

One week in Bible study, there it was: our memory verse for the week. Romans 8:14, "For all who are led by the Spirit of God are children of God." The next week, she said as she introduced the lesson, "Sandy, here is verse you might want to learn." Our memory verse was Ephesians 1:5, "God decided in advance to *adopt* us into His own family by bringing us to Himself through Jesus Christ. This is what he wanted to do, and it gave Him pleasure" (emphasis added).

For me, if God adopted me, then why should I feel I was not good enough for anyone to love me? *He adopted me.* I began to see my adoption as a good thing. It had nothing to do with someone not wanting me but doing for me what was best. That is true love. One who will make sacrifices for another's good is a living example of God's love. And those who are able to pick up that mantle of love likewise are extraordinarily loving people. Yes, I am blessed beyond measure and have an absolutely wonderful family, here and up there. Praise Him! And thank you, Mrs. Coffer.

Do everything without grumbling or arguing, so that
you may become blameless and pure; children of God
without fault in a warped and crooked generation.
—Philippians 2:14–15 NIV

THE TALE OF AN AVOCADO TREE

While visiting my friend Judy in California, we sat on her deck, and I noticed this magnificent, tall, sturdy, fruit-laden avocado tree. I commented that it was one of the prettiest trees I had ever seen. Judy smiled and told me the tale of this great tree.

Several years ago, when California suffered through some very severe El Nino storms, this tree suffered a terrible ordeal. Avocado trees have a shallow root system, and as storm after storm pounded Escondido, the ground became totally saturated. One afternoon, yet another storm filled with water and wind struck, and this beautiful, ten-year-old, heavily laden tree lost its footing and was upended with its roots exposed.

Initially, the plan was to take a chain saw to the tree. Fortunately, a neighbor told her that it might be possible to save the tree if she could replant and right the tree. Judy and her husband put out the word, and friends came to help with the rescue effort.

The first step was to severely prune the tree and cut away its sprawling canopy. Next, they winched the tree upright and replanted it. Finally, they added six strengthening posts to hold it in place.

Immediately, the forlorn tree went into deep shock, dropped all of its leaves and fruit, and stood naked and bare to weather yet more storms.

Several months passed, and Judy began to believe they had lost the battle to save the tree. As they contemplated cutting it down, they noticed a few leaf buds. Within a short time, new life burst forth with fine foliage, and by the next season, it was again bearing fruit. Only this time, it bore more fruit than it ever had before. Today, it has regained its majesty and continues to bear bumper crop after bumper crop of fruit.

As Judy told me this story, I thought about how, like the avocado tree, she too had weathered many storms. She was a breast cancer survivor and a recovered stroke victim. She faced many tragedies in her life, including watching a son suffer from an accident that left him paraplegic, having a mother stricken with Alzheimer's, and having a mother-in-law who suffered a painful terminal illness. Judy nursed them all and developed cardiac issues on top of it all.

Her life had been saturated with trials and tribulations; it had been upended and pruned. Fortunately, her husband and friends served as support beams as she regained her footing. She said that through each episode she gained new insight and knowledge that prepared her to help others and gave her a more empathetic understanding.

Today, Judy bears a bumper crop of goodness. She makes dozens of quilts for cancer patients, shares her home with foreign exchange students, is an activist for women's health issues, and stands ready to help whenever the phone rings. And it rings often. She is known as a generous and caring person.

The Good Gardner always prunes His plants. Otherwise, they grow without purpose and become feral. So when things seem like they can't get any worse, we should stop and thank God for pruning and upending us. For if we face no trials or tribulations, we too will grow with no purpose, and our crop of goodness will certainly diminish. At such times, we have but two choices. We can either roll about in the mud of self-pity or sink our roots deeper and prepare for the coming harvest.

"The Lord God made all kinds of trees
grow out of the ground—trees that were
pleasing to the eye and good for food."
—Genesis 2:9 NIV

SLURPING FROM THE SAUCER

In July, two of my daughters gave birth during the same week. While waiting for the first of the two births to occur, I met an excited and anxious woman pacing around the waiting room. I asked if her daughter was in labor. She nodded and told me that this was her first grandchild. I smiled and told her that I remembered how excited and nervous I was when my first grandchild was born and that the excitement never fades, regardless of how many times you experience the miracle of birth. In turn, she asked me how many grandchildren I had. Of course, being a grandmother, there is no greater joy than telling others about your little darlings. Also, I enjoyed answering this question because most people are so surprised at my answer. I informed her that I had twenty-one and was waiting for number twenty-two and that another daughter would be delivery number twenty-three later in the week. She paused a moment and said, "My, my, how wealthy you are."

Within minutes, my daughter was ready to deliver, and I was fortunate enough to witness the birth. By all standards, it was an easy birth, and Rebekah Annalee announced her arrival with a very loud squall.

Four days later, the labor/delivery room scenario was repeated. Only this time it was my eldest daughter giving birth to her fifth child.

About two hours into her labor, I visited the gift shop. There I found a cute teddy bear that I thought might be a good focal point for her when her labor intensified. As I paid for the teddy bear, the cashier asked if I had a new grandchild. I repeated my story of having two grandbabies being born in the same week and added the fact that this was number twenty-three. She smiled and said, "Oh! How your cup runneth over."

Again, after a relatively short and easy labor, I witnessed the birth of Jacob Reed, who greeted the world with soft coos. That afternoon as I drove home from the hospital, the words of the first-time grandmother and the cashier rang in my ears. Two times in one week, others had reminded me of how God blessed me. While I had prayed for safe deliveries and healthy babies, I only saw the births of these children as blessings for my daughters and their burgeoning families. I had been so wrapped up in the events surrounding the impending births that I failed to recognize how these wee ones were also blessings to me.

That night writing in my journal, I started to list the past week's blessings. Six pages later, I paused because of writer's cramp. Reviewing such an abundance of blessings, I felt overwhelmed. How could I not have acknowledged His blessings? With a contrite heart, I asked for His forgiveness for taking everything for granted. I praised His wondrous and generous nature. I thanked Him for answered prayers. I thanked Him for the new lives for Rebekah and Jacob and the delight and joy I received from all my grandchildren. Oh, yes, I am very wealthy—wealthy in the abundance of His love and blessings, and now I slurp from the saucer because my cup runneth over.

Therefore, their people turn to them and
drink up waters in abundance.
—Psalm 73:10 NIV

BRAID STRONG

While having a "sharing" breakfast with a large group of women who had just completed a thirty-week Bible study, a lady shared what the study meant to her. She spoke eloquently about the study itself and then turned to the point of the relationships that had developed during the study and how the study had been a thread that brought the women to a closer walk with God and one another.

I continued to listen carefully to each of those women who were sharing their experiences over the last year and noticed there really was a deep sense of building relationship with God and with one another and how the study had united them. My mind started to wander to another voice. I began to see how different ladies were affected. Some spoke of God's love and grace, others spoke of Jesus's willing sacrifice for our salvation, and one spoke of how the same Holy Spirit that was active in biblical times is the same Holy Spirit that we have within us, proffering power and strength. The three threads, God the Father, Jesus the Son, and the Holy Spirit.

Anyone who has had a daughter, or two, or three knows about the braid. I remember my first attempts were awkward. It didn't lay down properly, or it wasn't smooth or flat. Sometimes I had to repeatedly braid my daughter's hair. And heaven help me when we started doing the French braid. However, the three-strand central braid was critical to successfully completing the French braid.

So, what are the qualities of a braid? Each section is reliant upon the other to complete the braid. All get an equal chance at being the center strand. A braid is strong; it is flexible and impossible to break.

Have you ever been asked to explain the Trinity? The braid is a good example of the Holy Trinity. You have one head of hair, divided into three parts and braided together. You need each strand to make a braid. Each strand strengthens the braid.

When we study His Word, we learn about the different functions of the Trinity. As we grow in our study, we gain understanding, we gather knowledge, and we accumulate wisdom. Each verse we learn, each testimony we give, and each song of praise we sing become flowers in our bridal braid as we come to Him as His bride.

So, the next time you braid your hair or your daughter's, prayerfully consider the braid as an example of the Holy Trinity and rest assured His grace is upon you or your daughter. He walks alongside you or your daughter, and He fills you or your daughter with power. So turn the braid into a holy braid.

Therefore, go and make disciples of all nations,
baptizing them in the name of the Father
and of the Son and of the Holy Spirit,
—Matthew 28:29 NIV

The Mighty Colorado

When reflecting on events in one's life, it is helpful to select those that were defining moments. These are moments that either accelerated or became an obstacle in your life, spiritually, physically, or emotionally. Pondering this, one such event certainly stuck out in my memory. It was a life-or-death day.

Since we were living in a vacation destination (Hawaii), we looked forward to a vacation on the mainland. My thirtieth high school reunion was coming up in June 1990. Since we were attending it in Phoenix, Arizona, we wanted to take time and reconnect with several Arizona landmarks. It had been many years since we had been in Arizona. Over years past, I had been to the Grand Canyon many times but had never seen it from the bottom looking up. We decided to do a river raft trip. Our plan was to hike down, board our raft, and spend five glorious days on the river. We were advised that the canyon trails could be deceiving both in climbing out and going in. Our first fitness exercise would be to climb down the Kaibab Trail. It is a beautiful, steep, nine-mile downward trek that is absolutely brutal on one's knees, feet, and particularly toes. In preparation, we trained by hiking up and down Diamondhead several times a week.

All went well while visiting Phoenix. In addition to attending the reunion, we bought a house, knowing that our days of living in

Hawaii were ending. We were excited about getting to the canyon and meeting up with our guides. The informational meeting added to the allure of taking a roller-coaster ride for five days. The guide's closing words were, "This is not a Disney ride. Be careful. Listen to the engine. If it stops, be prepared to bail out upon my command. And finally, if you do have to bail out or if you fall out, turn your feet downstream. That way, your feet will take the knocks instead of your head."

We were up at dawn. The weather was wonderful. The vistas were breathtaking. We had adrenaline for breakfast. Each time we rounded a curve, we were awed by the canyon's beauty. The temperatures began to rise as we neared the bottom of the canyon. Little did we know Phoenix's temperatures were soaring. The first thing we did was to kick off our hiking boots and put our feet in the cold water of the Colorado. Our raft was waiting. It was a large pontoon raft. We set off. Again, looking at the canyon from the bottom truly gives a different perspective. It felt as if we were in a magnificent natural cathedral.

About two hours later, we landed on a small beach, and our first mate prepared a gourmet lunch. Satiated and eager to return to the river, we set off once more. We noticed when we waded out to board the raft that the water was extremely cold. Temperatures in Phoenix were reaching record height. Phoenix had to close Sky Harbor Airport because it was unsafe for planes to take off when temperatures were over 120°F. Glen Canyon was drawing water from the bottom of the reservoir where the water is the coldest to supply electricity demands of air-conditioning in Phoenix.

Sometime later, we pulled over before entering a class 5 rapids to allow the pilot of the raft and his first mate to scout the rapids to figure out what line we would enter the rapids. When they returned, the first mate remarked, "You are in for a ride. It's spitting vipers." From our point of view, we couldn't see the rapids. They double-checked our life jackets and told us no one could sit up on the pontoons. All must stay seated down in the boat.

With that, we shoved off and made a large, sweeping turn. There it was. A monster. The rapids were roiling and churning. We entered the rapids, and even though it was rough, I thought, *This isn't as bad as it looks.* Almost simultaneously, I looked up and saw a wave building until it reached a height high above my head. What a sight! I was so enraptured by the sight I felt no fear or apprehension. What happened in seconds was now in slow motion. My husband grabbed my hand and yelled, "We're going to dump!" The raft dipped dramatically and began to climb up the wave. And there was no sound from the engine. The pilot yelled something, and I couldn't distinguish what it was but knew we were in trouble. I was on the right of my husband, and I rolled across him and hit the water. It was peaceful now with the sun shimmering through the water. I could see bubbles escaping from my mouth, and I ate some river sand. I surfaced, drew a breath, and immediately was pulled back underwater. From peaceful to frightening, it was now dark. No sparkling sunlight filtered through the water. Disoriented, I flipped about like a fish out of water. (Pardon the cliché, but it fits perfectly.) Frantic realization sank in as I saw an enormous form with stuff hanging from its sides. It resembled a weirdly shaped octopus. Then came the realization. I was under the raft. I couldn't swim because the force of the churning water was too strong. So much for turning so my feet so they were headed downstream. I had no sense of direction. My body felt limp with no strength, just moving with the water. My lungs were screaming for air, and I knew then I was about to die.

Suddenly, I popped up above the water. I could breathe. That privilege lasted about thirty seconds, and then the water started to rise. I was once again under the water. About thirty seconds later, my head was above water again. I was in an air pocket near the front of our upside-down raft. And again and again and again, the water would rise, cover my head, and then slowly drop and go back down. I felt as if I was in a washing machine holding on to the agitator. Each time it happened, my body slammed against a boulder. I learned later we had capsized on the Big Red boulder in the middle of the river.

A memorable moment came with I heard my mother's voice as clear as if she was under the raft with me. This was particularly strange since she died in 1979. She said, "Cover your head, Sandy." This was repeated three times. I responded by pushing my head against the very hot metal bottom of the raft.

After nearly three hours, thereabouts, I heard someone walking on top of the boat calling, "Is anyone under there?" I yelled back before my head went under for another round of submersion. Thus began my rescue. I was growing weaker, and my hands were slipping off and on the bar I had been grasping. On a comic side, my rescuer told me to just hold on, the helicopter was on its way. My vision of that was they were going to lift the raft with the helicopter, and I would be hanging beneath the raft. Obviously, I was becoming confused in my thinking.

Shortly thereafter, another man was on top of the raft. He kept talking with me, keeping me calm. He passed a rope with a big knot on the end of it. I grabbed it, and he gave me two explicit instructions: (1) Do not wrap the rope around my hand; just hang on to it. (2) Upon his command, I was to drop down and slide beneath the "sissy bar," and they would pull me out. He tried to get my cooperation many times. I remember being terrified to leave the safety of the little air pocket. In a voice that sounded like God, he said, "Sandy, you are going to die under there unless you do what I say. We will try this again. On the number three, drop down and trust me to take it from there." With intense trepidation, on his count, I dropped down, and I don't remember him pulling me up, but I do remember being pulled onto a very, very hot raft bottom.

The saga is nearing its end. There was but one more hurdle to cross—taking a helicopter ride. I am terrified of helicopters. While living in Hawaii, there had been numerous helicopter crashes. I vowed I would *never* ride on a helicopter. Given the circumstances, no other options were available. While the helicopter hovered above, a paramedic was lowered. He called the hospital up on the canyon's South Rim to advise them of my vitals. I heard him tell them that I was hypothermic. I kept asking about my husband, and finally they told me that everyone was accounted for, whatever that meant.

The next step in the rescue process was getting me to the helicopter that hovered above. They put me in a net zip-up, one-piece romper, hooked me to a cable, and pulled me up to about thirty feet under the helicopter. As we swung out over the river, I was more terrified than I ever was beneath the raft. I became aware of a real draft. It was then I became aware that my shorts were gone, my shoes were gone, along with my unmentionables. I was flying across the river, with many canoes backed up because of the accident, in less attire than was acceptable. After I recovered from that bit information, I waited for them to pull me into the helicopter, but due to the updrafts and a bunch of other aeronautical terms, they let me dangle for a while. Obviously, I survived this ordeal. I was taken directly to the hospital, where later I was reunited with my husband. His first words to me were, "Ready to go again? Now that was a Triple E ticket ride."

Sometimes God needs to wake us up. I must have been pretty hardheaded. I had to face possibly losing my life before I realized that He wanted me to listen to Him, respond to Him, seek Him, and serve Him. During my brief stay at the hospital, I recalled this verse. I don't ever remember memorizing it or even hearing it before. Some years later, I came across it in the Bible. What a surprise that was. God gets his point across! Praise Him, and to Him alone be all glory and honor.

When you pass through the waters, I will be with
you; and through the rivers, they shall not overwhelm
you when you walk through fire you shall not be
burned, and the flame shall not consume you.
—Isaiah 43:2 NIV

A White Corsage

Oh, how I wish
    I could bring you flowers
        Or take you to lunch,
           And
    You would make me apple crisp
        And tell me about your life
           Before I came along.

Oh, how I wish
    I could hear your laughter
        And see those crinkles 'round your eye.
           And
    In the kitchen we could sit
        And sip some coffee and share our lives.

Oh, how I wish
    I could catch your fragrance in the air
        And feel the warmth of your embrace,
           And
    You could see your grandchildren
        And watch as their babies grow in grace.

Oh, how I wish
    I could hear your voice
        Or stroke your soft, smooth hands,
          And
    We go swimming once again
        And stop to feed those little cactus wrens.

Today and every day
    I remember your watchful and tender care,
        your words of wisdom,
        and the bond we shared.
I remember also the tears you shed,
        your sleepless nights,
        your fears, and all that dread.
I remember, most, your zest for life,
        your passion for Dad,
        and your love for me.

On this your special day,
    I shall, once again, wear a white corsage
        And try not to envy those who wear colored flowers.
    I shall recall our days together, both tumultuous and serene,
        And recognize your selflessness and sacrifice supreme.
    I shall look toward heaven
        And know that you've found your place
           Somewhere between greeting new arrivals
           And polishing the pearly gates.
    I shall pause and touch the plaque that bears your name
        And delight when the carillon and organ play.
    I shall think of you with all the angels and their harps
        Praising God with "How Great Thou Art."
    I shall walk through the church kitchen
        And remember your service there
           Of countertops scrubbed

And food prepared.
I shall share memories of you
So all may know
That you walked in His light
As far as you could go.

And one day,
I, too, shall join you,
And together we shall rejoice
At what was bound here on earth
Shall ever be,
And we shall bask in the light of His love.

Until then,
Happy Mother's Day!

Honor your father and your mother, as the Lord your
God has commanded you, so that your days may
be prolonged and so that it may go well with you
in the land which the Lord your God gives you.
—Deut. 5:16 AMP

PERSPECTIVES AND PRIORITIES

Although it doesn't seem possible, another year is winding down. Before we know it, we will be knee deep in the holiday season with all of its parties, decorations, feasts, and family gatherings. I used to believe that the older you become, the faster time passes. The only truth in that is the part about growing older. It happens, folks. Aging is a process. Time doesn't change. There remain twenty-four hours per day, each day of each year. Nothing changes. So, why do the years seem to go faster?

The reason it appears to go so fast is subliminally obvious. As stores put out Halloween merchandise in July, Thanksgiving things in August, and Christmas decorations in early September, the year feels shortened by at least three months. I can remember when Mother used to complain at seeing Christmas decorations being put up immediately after Thanksgiving. Now, Valentine cards are in the rack before the after-Christmas sales have even begun.

From Martin Luther King Day through Christmas, newspapers, television ads, pop-up text ads, and inboxes are crammed full of super-mega sale specials. For a large segment of the population, the holidays are simply fun days filled with shopping trips and sporting events. For many, the holidays have lost their true meaning. When was the last time you went to a Memorial Day service at a cemetery? Whatever happened to the grand parades on Easter and St. Patrick's Day? Most have slipped into oblivion due to poor attendance.

I recently asked my teenage grandson what he knew about Veteran's Day. His eyes glazed over, and he got that "What's with you, Grandma?" look on his face and just shrugged his shoulders. "Do we get out of school?" was his only response. It might be interesting to find out how many people really do understand the importance of Veteran's Day. Its significance is being lost. In fact, many employers give employees the option to bypass Veteran's Day so that they can take time off for those infamous Black Friday sales (a.k.a. day-after-Thanksgiving sales). As a sidebar, as more stores open on Thanksgiving, more and more people will leave their homes after they have had Thanksgiving dinner to shop at the Black Friday sales than will go to the polls and vote. This is truly a picture of materialism.

Given today's political tone and correctness, we could probably pass a law to rename our holidays. For example, how about Super Bowl Widows Shopping Day, the Great Guys in History Sales, the Horsey Derby Day, Indy Speedway Shopping Day, the Firecracker Specials Day, the Workers Shopping Holiday, the World Series of Values, the Blow Out and Best-Ever Holiday Day, and there is the Post-Holiday Sale for any day we might have missed. Being aware of what is happening within our society and government is important to our long-term benefit. Hmmm, is there a holiday for that?

It has been said that religion is the opiate of the people. What a lie! Great civilizations have fallen into ruin not over religion but because their citizens devalued their country's history and its leader. They became increasingly humanistic and chose to live a more hedonistic lifestyle of self-absorption. When people are preoccupied with their need for self-gratification and narcissistic behaviors (such is the *shop till you drop* mentality), they lose contact with their core values of spiritual awareness. The opiate of narcissism is a high that requires constant feeding.

Holidays should be a reflection of what is important to us as a nation and as families. Perhaps it is time to slow down the year by taking time to explain to our children the importance of those special days. We need to refocus our energy and reclaim our identity by remembering that holidays are more than days off for shopping or sporting events. Instead, share with them the vision of a civil rights leader, honor great presidents, give pause to remember those brave men and women who died for our freedom and right to vote, celebrate the birth of this grand republic and its stand against tyranny, recognize the efforts of the working person, acknowledge the courage of an explorer, give honor to all who have and do serve in the military, thank God for the end of World War II and for His bountiful blessings, and celebrate God's plan for eternal salvation through the birth of His Son, Jesus. If we undermine these holidays by making them more and more secular and commercial, we will lose both our cultural and spiritual identities.

We need to spend time with our young people, sharing our heritage and our beliefs with them. They will not learn them from shopping, watching sports, or playing computer games. Holidays are days of respite. Respite equals rest, and rest equals a peaceful time. Enjoy your family. Have a real holiday. You might even feel that time has slowed.

We will not hide them from their children, but [we will] tell to the generation to come the praiseworthy deeds of the Lord, and [tell of] His great might and power and wonderful works He has done.
—Psalm 78:4 AMP

A Sweet, Sweet Memory

For months, our family planned our trip to Arizona to visit Grandma and Grandpa. There is nothing quite like a road trip to enliven your life, particularly with four children under the age of ten. I have often wondered if our trip was an inspiration for Chevy Chase's. Who can forget *National Lampoon's Vacation*?

Our trip was moderately uneventful. We heard the infamous "Are we there yet?" at least ten times an hour. There were the sibling skirmishes. "Rolland farted." "Monika hit me." "Heidi pinched me." And the youngest, Erika, just wailed when something was amiss. We tried to keep the children entertained and bribed with snacks, road games such as looking at license plates, hand games, comic books, and silly songs such as "Little Rabbit Foo Foo." For the most part, they were pretty well behaved, and we tended to travel late mornings into late evening. Oh, how I loved to see the sun go down, because the children tended to go down as well.

We made an exception on the Fourth of July in 1974. We decided we needed to make it to Colorado Springs before nightfall because we wanted to be in a larger city in order to go to the fireworks display. The children always loved the display, and July Fourth was a big holiday in our family. It always included a picnic at the display site.

We rolled into Colorado Springs around three thirty in the afternoon, found a motel, and had the little girls, Heidi and Erika, take a nap, while my husband found out where the display would be and got driving instructions. Believe it or not, there was no GPS yet. Soon it was time to leave. Fortunately, there was a Kentucky Fried Chicken on the road to the display. We got our usual bucket of original chicken and three large cartons of coleslaw and biscuits with honey. I shuddered to think what sticky, greasy, naturally dirty, messy kids I would have by the time we got back to the motel. But wasn't that the fun of it all?

We arrived, pulled out some old blankets, and marched resolutely into the park, locating what we believed to be the perfect spot. We spread the blankets, broke out the picnic, and sat back to relax for a great evening.

Rolland was first to see the dark, moving mass coming toward us in the sky. "Mom, what's that?" I looked up and didn't really recognize what it was. And just as I was about to answer him, something broke away from the mass and dive-bombed right at me. Oh, no. It was a bat. *This is the Fourth of July, not Halloween*, I thought. Soon, the bats were dive-bombing everyone there. There were shrieks, yells, and people waving their arms, things, blankets, fold-up chairs, anything they could at the rampaging critters. Mayhem! Chaos! I tried to cover the younger girls with my arms. My husband looked like a papa eagle with his arms flung out from his sides, trying to shield the older children. He yelled to me, "If this doesn't stop soon, we need to pack up and leave." That set off strident, nearly hysterical yelps of disagreement from the children. "No, no, no, Daddy!" They had been closed up in a car for nearly three days, and this outing was joyous freedom.

The bat brigades continued to swarm around. They seemed to have more than a mild interest in the closed bucket of chicken. We withstood their irritating attack for a couple more minutes, and my husband was definitely growing more irritated and impatient. He started to gather up the food. When he stood up, I noticed our three-year-old, Erika, was kneeling in the middle of the blanket. Her hands were folded, and her face was looking upward. Then I heard her sweet little voice, "God, please make the 'ats' go away." She just remained kneeling and looking heavenward, and amazingly, the bats did not go near her. Within a couple of minutes, there wasn't a bat in the sky. Thus, Erika was designated as our little hotline to heaven.

Never in my life do I remember feeling the absolute joy and such deep humility as that of seeing my young child express her belief and faith in God. It is an indelible memory that I can close my eyes today, forty-plus years later, and still remember. Thank you, Lord.

"Let the children come to me and do not hinder
them, for to such belongs the kingdom of heaven."
—Matthew 19:14 ESV

Printed in the United States
By Bookmasters